Kennel Ideas

4th Edition

Kennel Ideas

4th Revised Edition

A collection of clever ideas and
tricks-of-the-trade on dog kenneling
that will save you time, trouble and money

by Victoria Webb Cartner

4th Revised Edition

Published by
Farmington Publishing
1485 Powell Road
Woodleaf, NC 27054

Library of Congress Catalog Card
Number 98-94797

Printed in the United States of America

ISBN 0-9618992-3-9

Contents

Introduction

Whether you are an inexperienced dog keeper of limited means and knowledge or an experienced breeder who is still open for new ideas, to raise dogs and do it successfully you must constantly be on the lookout for new ideas and ways to improve what you already have.

In 1986 I knew that I had to build a new kennel. I frantically combed the bookstores for the book that would tell me exactly what I needed to know to begin construction. I thought that surely someone with years of experience would have compiled a reference book for those that wanted to build their own kennel.

Knowing that I myself did not have the expertise, I wrote a letter to the editors of the major dog magazines asking for their reader's help. Within a few days after the issues hit the newsstands, the letters and cards started rolling in. Individuals responded from all over the United States and Canada telling me what kind of kennel they had built, what worked and what didn't work. They gave me ideas on everything from building a kennel to the best tools needed to get the job done right. Though many people submitted the same ideas, many came through with unique tips and provided the information for this book to share with other kennel owners.

That was 1986. Since then we have reprinted revised editions every few years, updating phone numbers and addresses, where necessary and adding new information.

In exchange for their ideas I promised a free copy of the next edition. The offer still stands. If you have a tip that you can share, certainly let us know.

We have included a loose sheet of internet sites you may want to check out. Since they change so often we decided to insert updated versions as we mail out each book.

No one can tell you what kind of kennel is best for you. There are too many personal factors involved. This book is intended merely to offer suggestions and to show you some ways of making your dogs comfortable and reduce to a minimum the labor involved in the chores of caring for them.

I hope this book will prove invaluable as a reference tool and that by reading ideas submitted by others that you can improve on what already exists.... perhaps making day to day life for your dog more pleasant in some way.

vc

Kennel Ideas from Other Breeders

Lee A. Wolfe
High Point, North Carolina *Dalmations*

Lee had just finished building a small kennel to house his dalmations when he submitted this information. The entire kennel is 12x32 feet with each of his four runs measuring 8x12 feet.

The sides are 6 foot chain link fencing with a 32 inch gate in the front of each run. Aluminum roofing was used so that the kennel would be cooler in the summer and warmer in the winter. Aluminum is also light-weight, but very rigid and won't rust. On the floor he used 2x4 inch mesh wire so that the dogs couldn't dig out. This is covered with "screening", a powdered gravel that is clean and packs down fairly hard. This type of powdered gravel is very economical (around $4 per ton). It won't stick to the dog's coat like sand does. It is also good on the dogs' paws and stays cool in the sun.

Lee built wooden 2x4 decks, which are raised off the ground with bricks for ventilation and for the dogs to lie on at night when it's too hot to sleep in their dog houses. Each dog house is double-walled, with insulation between the walls.

Kennel Ideas

A wooden sun screen is located on the southwestern side of the kennel where the sun sets. This also keeps the dogs cool, providing shade, but allowing light through also

Gloria Lewis
Closter, New Jersey

Miniature Schnauzers

Gloria maintains from 5 to 10 dogs, including pups, breeding on the average of one litter per year. She converted the lower level of her home into a place for housing the dogs. One room is utilized for large crates in which the dogs are confined, while the other room is used as a den by the family, allowing the dogs "couch" privileges.

Adjacent to the den is the utility room which contains a sink for bathing. A separate grooming room opens to the outside runs.

There are 3 runs which are about 4 feet wide and go the length of the property, approximately 1/3 of an acre. The runs connect to a fenced patio which is covered with rigid vinyl as protection against rain and hot sun. A separate, smaller pen is adjacent. The whole back yard is fenced with privacy stockade fencing in which the dogs are permitted to run. The long runs are covered with pea gravel.

Runs and patio are hosed daily with a mixture of Clorox and water, attached to a spray nozzle and run through the outside hose. A central vacuum system helps keep the quarters clean.

Kennel Ideas

Dorothy B. Israel
Birdsong Gordon Setters
Soiling Springs, Pennsylvania

Gordon Setters

In order to make her workshop/study double as both a whelping and puppy room, Dorothy decided to make her home her kennel, with her 3 dogs living in intimate contact with her daily life.

Crates are in various areas of the house, with one room set aside for the purpose of a whelping room and nursery for several months at a time. Since that room's ordinary function is a leather crafts workshop, grooming room and her own all-purpose study, it is filled with paraphernalia for various purposes.

Puppy-proofing the room would be a major undertaking if all of the tools and materials, usually stored there on shelves, bins, etc., had to be removed. During her last litter she came up with a successful solution, arousing interest from neighbors and other breeders.

In effect, she fenced out the room. Portable panels from 2x4's were built and medium-duty fence fabric (welded 2x4 inch wire) stapled to them. Each panel fitted one wall of the room and was custom-sized to allow reasonably easy access to the material that was stored behind it, along the wall.

The panels were linked to each other by a simple hook & eye and were quite stable. Because of the open fence fabric, access to the wall receptacles was not limited. This idea made a January whelping, which required heat lamps, heating pads and auxiliary heaters, a blessing! She was able to get to the work table drawers, the few times she needed something special, whereas previous arrangements, with plywood sheets, had prevented such access. Best of all, it was easy and lightweight working with the panels. When disassembled, they were quite easy to store.

Kennel Ideas

Olivia Johnson
One O'Clock Whippets
North Platte, Nebraska

Whippets

Olivia Johnson wrote to submit her "dream" dog room. Raising 2 or 3 whippet litters a year and preferring to keep her population small, she designed this kennel so that a separate kennel building would not be necessary. She did, however, want to keep all of her show, dog and feeding supplies in one place, separate from the dogs.

She designed this diagram which contains an adequate, yet minimal amount of accessories.

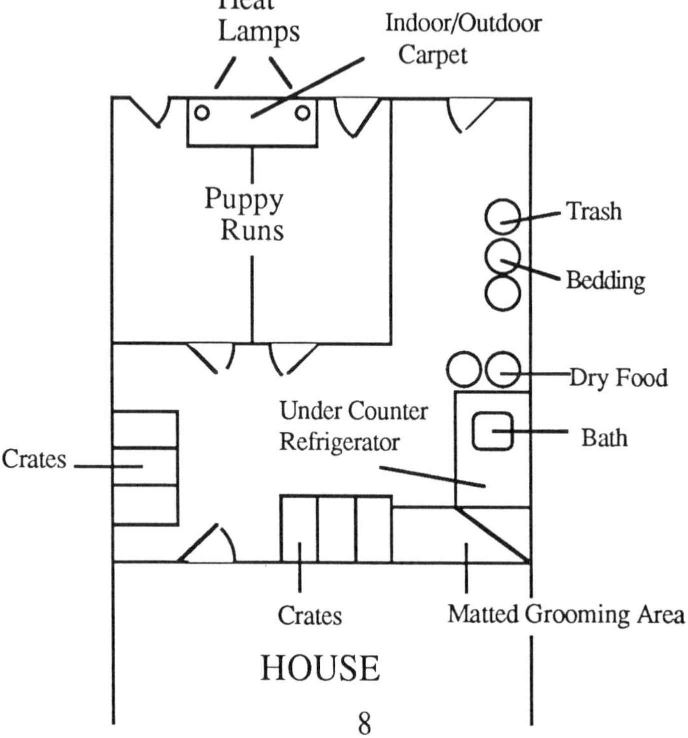

Plastic trash cans are utilized for holding dry puppy or adult food, trash & soiled dog laundry. Her crates are all the same size for easy organization except for a couple of smaller ones that stack. She personally prefers all-wire cages so the dogs have visual contact with each other.

Under-the-counter space holds medicine, grooming supplies, dog food cans & dishes, in addition to a small refrigerator for perishables, including vaccines & puppy milk. A hand-held shower is a must for bathing in an oversized sink. A securing chain attached to the wall to hold them still is also included. The entire counter should be covered in rubber matting or carpeting for better footing.

The puppies are whelped in the house in a spare bedroom in a large cardboard box. Her small breed takes a big TV box. The litter lives here until about 3 1/2 weeks old. At that age they find out how to open the door and the bitch no longer cleans up after them.

There is a small door cut in one end of the rectangle, high enough to make the bitch "hop in" and since it's only cut on three sides, the flap can be pushed up to keep puppies in and drafts out.

With a heat lamp, designed for baby pigs, suspended above, it is easy to keep the pups warm. The high cardboard sides insulate against drafts. The traditional swimming pools for kids or wooden pens lack this quality. While the heavier coated breeds may do just fine with the latter, hers are extremely subject to chill because of their short coats and lack of fat on their bodies. The bottom of the box is lined with several pads of newspaper, under a blanket, making cleaning only a matter of minutes. The box is easily disposed of when no longer needed.

From here the pups go to a commercial central, metal play pen for a couple of weeks. Weather permitting, they are later placed outside or to an indoor exercise pen for winter litters.

The most desirable choice of bedding, in her opinion, is cedar shavings, held in by a couple of planks along the bottom. Despite the occasional scare of eye injury, many fellow breeders raise hundreds of pups this way with no problems. "It certainly is the cleanest and easiest" says Olivia. Litter care is extremely time consuming and quick clean-up really helps out.

In her layout, each puppy section opens to private play yards because it is almost imperative to keep young ones away from larger adults and even older pups. Play is simply too rough and babies suffer temperamentally from being continuously picked on. The indoor sections could be either wood with welded wire, commercial runs or free standing pens.

Kimberly Beezel
Von Cameron Shepherds
Hepzibah, West Virginia

German Shepherds

Kimberly lives in West Virginia and points out that they have all types of imaginable weather, from very cold and below zero, to hot and humid.

She built her kennel in 1982 laying the concrete pad first, 20 feet wide by 30 feet long. A storage building was put on one end measuring 10x10 feet. Six foot chain link fencing was attached to this for the kennels.

The kennels are 5x20 feet. The posts for the chain link fencing were set in concrete as it was being poured. A slope on the concrete allows the surface to dry quickly after hosing.

Doors were added at the end of the kennels which were 5 feet wide. She discovered, however, that they are much too wide as they constantly slip. Every month or so she has to adjust them. She now recommends only a 2 to 2 1/2 foot wide door. This would leave less chance for a dog to escape.

Hinges on the doors are such that they swing in either direction, adding to their versatility.

A concrete sidewalk and drain was later poured along the 3 sides of the kennel, deepening the trough on the low end of the slope so that the water drains off.

The drainage goes into a 55 gallon drum that is placed underground with 3 inches of gravel below it and 3 inches of gravel in the bottom of the barrel. "Limnate" digester chemicals, which work well when directions are followed, are used. Make sure that you begin using "Limnate" when the weather will be at least 75 degrees or more for a period of 3 to 4 days. Kimberly said she erroneously started it in the fall and once summer arrived, had a messy "bailing out" job to do.

Three and a half years after first building her kennel she expanded. Not wanting to invest a large sum of money on materials and concrete, she improvised. For the two additional kennels, also measuring 5x20 feet, she used some 4 foot tall chain link fencing purchased at an auction. For posts, 4x4 wolmanized (treated) lumber was used. Used gates were picked up reasonably through yard sales. The floor of these kennels consists of 2 inches of medium gravel on the ground with a sufficient supply of hay or straw on top of that so as to keep the dogs feet from getting sore. Of course, these two kennels must be manually scooped for cleanliness.

Kimberly also adds that she definitely prefers concrete, for several reasons, among them, cleanliness and no chance of injury to dog paws by straw or rocks imbedding in their pads. One dog had to have surgery to extract straw and gravel chips that got in the pad of her foot. The chips cut it and caused an infection. "Though some people don't like concrete because they feel it breaks down the bone and muscles over a period of time and causes calluses on elbows when the dog lies down, I feel like any type of flooring will have its drawbacks as well as advantages". Though concrete is more expensive at the onset, it is cheaper in the long run because you have healthier dogs as a result of being able to detect a change in stools, such as consistency or worms. Fewer fleas and other insect problems are noted on concrete as well as being able to notice a female coming into "heat" more easily. Male dogs don't seem to pick up the "heat" scent as easily either on concrete, according to Kimberly, especially neighborhood strays.

In the construction of all 4 kennel runs, labor was done solely by friends and relatives. Chain link fencing was stretched also by themselves...Hard to do, but not impossible! She indicated that it turned out strong and very stable.

The last two kennels, which were added later, were constructed with outside help with the condition that Kimberly be there to help and act as "gopher", finding the nails, hammer, etc. when necessary.

As for the dog houses, one is a galvanized steel, insulated one, which she prefers for cleanliness, simplicity, and insulating qualities. The other three were built of lumber scraps, of which one is an A-frame. The A-frame house wastes a lot of space and is too heavy to lift to clean underneath. It takes 3 large men to lift it.

The chain link fencing is 11 gauge, with a 1 1/2 inch mesh. Given the opportunity again, however, Kimberly says she would choose 1 inch mesh. At that size the dogs cannot chew and disfigure the chain link or risk broken teeth, dog nose bites or paws getting caught.

As for whelping and puppy ideas she offered these hints: For a first-time mother, she uses a whelping box which is 4x4 feet in the laundry room of her home. On bitches that have safe, normal deliveries and have had a previous litter, she lets them stay outside in the doghouse where they are more at home. The exception is during weather which is too cold for whelping and newborn pups. These bitches are checked every 30 minutes or so, just in case trouble occurs.

Yvette S. Bonner
Thanksgiving Acres
Kemp, Texas

Shih Tzu's

After building a small kennel with a combination whelping/puppy room, Yvette submitted a description of her kennel layout and ideas on raising dogs.

The main building is 12x40 feet. It is set on concrete which goes out beyond the south side (long side) four feet and then drops down onto grass in the runs which are forty feet long and divided every four feet across.

Since she breeds only Shih Tzu's and they are a toy breed and very compatible with each other, she left off dividing all the indoor-outdoor runs. Instead, only every other run is divided. As her drawing shows, the dotted lines are where a chain link divider fence could be. On top of the chain link, which is set in concrete between the runs, she uses small (1 inch) chicken wire to stop any fence climbing.

Cages are 3x4 feet and made of wood and 1 inch chicken wire. They open outward with two small doors allowing her to reach into the far corners easily. These cages are floored with stiff bathroom sheeting board which is easily cleaned and washed. She uses these cages, which stack firmly on top of each other, for whelping boxes. Because the wood is not even with the floor of each cage, the puppies do not get suffocated or laid on since the wire "gives". These cages give plenty of room for the mothers to get away from their puppies during the day. She considers this crucial since many dams show signs of being upset by constantly being in with their pups. She lets the mothers out three or four times a day for some peace and quiet. Since they live out on a farm, she lets them out to run in the pasture and walk with her. It keeps them all happy and exercised and they are then ready to go back and be "mom" again.

Litters are kept in these cages until they are six weeks old. The cages are big enough for up to 5 young pups to be weaned in. Mothers-to-be are accustomed to these cages one week before they are due to whelp. Lots of newspapers are used on the floors, which are shredded by the bitch and made into a nest. Papers and cages are cleaned daily with a disinfectant cleanser.

Windows, in the kennel building, slide up and down with mesh screening. These allow a nice breeze. A box fan, in one end of the building, circulates the air and keeps it cool in the summer.

The outside perimeter fencing is a wooden privacy fence. It provides security, plus, it cuts down on barking because it restricts the dogs vision. The wooden perimeter fence is also set in concrete to stop digging out by Yvette's dogs and digging in by others.

The building is the height of a normal house. The walls and ceiling are heavily insulated and sheet rocked. Bathroom sheeting is used around the bottom of the walls. With the use of two oil heaters, that look like accordions, she is able to keep the dogs kenneled outdoors, at approximately 70 degrees in the winter. Puppies, between the ages of newborn to 4 weeks old, are kept in a constant temperature of 75 to 80 degrees.

An evaporative cooler is used for summertime cooling. Coolers such as these are typically used in dry cleaners and can be obtained from heating & air conditioning dealers. It keeps the kennel between 75 to 80 degrees even in the Texas heat.

The outside of the building is sheet paneling, making it look rather like a frame house. The roof is rolled roofing. The concrete floor has been slightly sloped and on the south side, where the dogs go out into the yard areas, there is about a 2 inch difference between the wall and floor to allow washing of the floor. This, however, is not enough, since dirt and hair get trapped in the opening and clogs it up, making more frequent cleaning a must.

Kennel Ideas

Shirley A. Hiatt
Bandit's Bassets
Havelock, North Carolina Basset Hounds

According to Shirley Hiatt, the greatest whelping box she's used is a child's plastic wading pool. Being plastic, it is leak proof and can be easily cleaned with disinfectants. Layers of newspapers are put in the bottom and changed when needed. Bitches can get in and out easily and pups stay put until well over 3 weeks old. Sides are high enough to keep out drafts for her Basset Hounds.

Should a wooden whelping box be preferred, Shirley recommended a drop door be added and covered with carpet so that the pups could walk up and down the ramp with good footing. The door can be kept shut, when necessary, with a sliding bolt, to keep the pups in.

Another idea which became very helpful with her last two litters, was savng flannel baby receiving blankets. By folding them in half and sewing them like a pillowcase, they can be slipped over heating pads, etc. The flannel blankets are soft, easily slipped off for washing and puppies don't get their nails caught in them like regular towels. The open end is fastened with safety pins, although Velcro strips would perhaps be quicker. Flannel blankets, such as these, can readily be picked up at a yard sale and used item baby shops, quite inexpensively.

In order to effectively clean the blankets, once soiled, Shirley uses cold water and 1/2 cup of a product like "Spic & Span" floor cleanser along with regular soap to take out most of the blood and stool stains.

Kennel Ideas

Sandra K. Martin
Sandamar Collies
Mexico, Missouri

Collies

Sandra's kennels were built around 1983. Kennel runs were made of 52" high and 16 foot long combination panels available from farm supply stores. Combination panels were used because they were easily accessible, no freight charges were necessary, they could be hauled on a 12 to 16 foot trailer or 2 to 3 at a time in a pick-up truck, bowed end to end with the tailgate shut. By building runs in this manner, they can be lengthened, shortened or added on to, to suit your budget or convenience.

Combination panels are easy to cut with a hacksaw (although it takes some time unless you have help to cut very many) and are quick to put up. They come in either 36 or 52 inch heights. Sandra chose the 52 inch height since, although her collies were not "jumpers" outside dogs, wanting in, may be.

Gates could also be made out of the panels. Red Top panels (approximately $20 each) are better in her opinion than Silver (approximately $14 to $18 each) because they have more cross wires for strength and durability.

Metal posts were spaced 8 feet apart. Corners were laced with wire for added strength. One panel was cut to allow for adjustments necessary with the 36 inch gates she chose. The gates were chain link in a pipe frame, bought second-hand from a breeder who was dismantling his kennel in favor of full-time judging. Extra posts were needed at the gates.

Two 8x32 foot runs and one 16x32 foot run were built with the 16 foot run designed for later division with additional 16x32 foot panels.

Between the three runs, 48 inch high chicken wire was attached to the panels to prevent fighting through the fence.

In order to provide a windbreak and shade, straw was stacked around the house end of the runs in the winter and sunflowers planted along the panels in the summer. Cedar trees were planted on the north and west sides providing for future shade.

Gravel & dirt were used for flooring except around gate areas. Flat river rock was hauled in and layed in a flagstone pattern for these areas. Gaps were filled with pea gravel. The rocks packed down rapidly to a tight fit, yet were able to be pried up with a shovel, with little effort, whenever modifications were necessary.

To keep from walking in mud in wet weather, a wall was constructed approximately 3 feet out from the front fenced run and the area in between filled with gravel. Landscape or railroad timbers work equally well. In order to facilitate the run off of water during heavy rains, 3 trenches were dug running the length of the runs and filled with large gravel.

Placement of the dog houses should be well thought out. Sandra had one athletic bitch who jumped on her doghouse and then over the fence.

Donna Metzler
St. Clairsville, Ohio

Since Donna has one dog that does not like to be on wet, muddy ground, as do neither most dogs, she came up with the following idea.

Concrete building blocks are laid end to end on their sides to make a base. Black rubber mats, used to keep cows from slipping in dairy barns, are put over the blocks.

Dogs are kept above the ground in this manner, and the rubber mats are easily cleaned. Since fencing goes to the bottom of the blocks, any digging out is prevented. This method would be best used for dogs not prone to chewing the rubber mats.

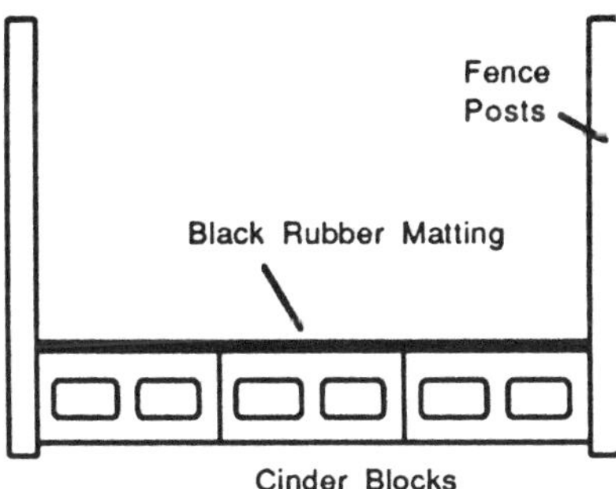

Kennel Ideas

J. Johnston
Nashville, Tennessee

Golden & Flat
Coated Retrievers

An innovative dog house, ideal for hot climates, has a flat roof that raises up or lowers, as needed according to Mr. Johnston.

To accomplish this, the underside of the roof has 4 to 6 wooden blocks which, when in a crosswise position, hold up the roof and create ventilation. When turned lengthwise, the roof goes down, level with the walls of the doghouse to cut off drafts.

Mr. Johnston feels that whelping boxes should never be made of wood or other material that cannot be disinfected adequately. "Parvo germs, for one, stay virile and deadly in wood and open ground for a minimum of 2 years." The best disinfectant according to Mr. Johnston's vet is about a 1/6th dilution of Clorox to 5/6ths water. The surface then needs to be thoroughly washed in plain water and dried before allowing subsequent contact by the dogs.

When building a dirt-bottomed puppy pen he had the builder set the fencing into a 10 inch ditch which was then filled with concrete. This prevented any possible digging out.

Minta L. Roper
Bob Burns
Dallas, Texas

Chows

This kennel was originally used for a goat pen. Chain link fencing was used with pipe run along the top. Though Chows aren't fence jumpers, they also had both a Doberman and a Shepherd that were. The pipe apparently made the dogs think twice, since they have never attempted to jump it.

By having a third of an acre in which to enjoy, all the dogs get to get out and run separately when it is time to clean the runs, feed and water. The main pair of dogs are allowed out in the evening, in this area, to run until the next morning.

Plywood was used in the construction process because it is so versatile. The roof on the shed was built of plywood, sealed, painted and then coated with roof pitch (tar) to prevent leaking in wet weather.

Runs measure 20 feet long by 15 feet wide. From the gatepost back to the building is a fence and another gate which enables one to either open the run totally, or separate the pen by closing the gate. Chain link fencing was not set in cement, so Minta found nailing a board at the bottom keeps pups and older dogs from digging or pushing under the fence. Plastic pipe runs across the top, about 6 to 8 inches above the chain link fencing.

Gates were made of plywood after being sealed and painted to discourage warping. Hook & eye latches are used on each side of the gate.

Pallets covered with plywood keep dogs up off of damp ground. In order to keep small pups from crawling underneath, the pallets were boxed in on the sides with boards.

A tie-down ring came in handy for a bitch who refused to nurse her pups after her first litter. She had to be leashed to the ring and supervised the first two weeks while her pups nursed. Minta's chows were very protective of their pups and the nursery had to be completely closed with solid partitions to prevent fighting through the fence.

With dirt flooring in the runs, cleanliness is maintained by simply raking everything out of the run. A layer of hay in the winter, especially under the pallets, holds in the warmth. Straw works best, if available.

Minta has since moved and is in the process of building again. Except for a few minor changes, she plans to use the same principles, since they seem to work for her.

Debbie Lackey
Sundance Pomeranians
Kerrville, Texas

Pomeranians

The first kennel Debbie had was small, only 14x16 feet, and was built at the same time as her home, by the same contractor. It was not fancy, but ended up costing approximately $2,000 compared to her much larger 24x36 foot new kennel which was built for only $2,500.

After dealing with contractors on the prior home and kennel, she decided to do her own contracting on the new one. A local carpenter was hired and local lumberyards were contacted to see if their scrap lumber piles could be gone through. Most of her wood was therefore obtained at a very cheap price. Kitchen cabinets, for storage, were obtained as rejects for only $25 each because of nicks & scratches on them from shipping.

Since she raises a small breed of dog, expensive chain link fencing was not necessary. Instead, 2x4 inch welded wire, in 50 foot rolls, was bought. A used, suspended, 100,000 BTU propane heater was purchased to heat the kennel and does an excellent job.

The dogs have 4x8 foot runs and 10x14 foot outdoor runs. These are connected by the "Magnador"brand mini dog doors. Cat boxes are used as beds filled with old sheets for bedding. Large plastic selfwaterers are in each pen, providing the dogs with plenty of water. Large self-feed rabbit feeders are used for food in each run. By using these feeders, they can be fed from outside the pen and can eat whenever they desire.

When feeding canned food, cheap paper plates are used. After trying stainless steel and plastic dishes, not only are the paper plates less expensive, but they save so much time spent previously washing & disinfecting. The plates are picked up immediately after the dog finishes, and tossed in the garbage to prevent shredding by bored dogs.

As the manager of a cleaning supply store, Debbie knows quite a bit about cleaning after 8 years on the job. The most important thing in a kennel is sealing the concrete if it is used for flooring. If the concrete is not sealed, it will flake, powder, sweat and absorb everything that is put on it. A good commercial sealer from a store such as hers, a hardware store or lumberyard will work. A good epoxy base paint also makes the concrete look good and makes it easier to clean. Water-based latex paint doesn't stay down in her opinion.

Though a lot of people use Clorox as a cleaner, Debbie recommends a good disinfectant cleaner instead, which is made to do the job. They cost about $7 per gallon and dilute at approximately 2 ounces per gallon of water, on the average. When runs are hosed down, a floor squeegee should be used to help dry the surface.

Large 3 x 3 foot rabbit hutches are used as whelping cages and puppy pens. They have pans to catch droppings and can be stacked 3 high. For a small breed of dog, they are perfect! Large breed sized crates are also good. They can be stacked for more room and some are inexpensive depending on where you get them.

A large 33 gallon Rubbermaid "Brute" trash can, with a top, is used to store dog food. It stays dry, is easy to get to, stays clean and no rodents or insects can penetrate it.

Two separate 12x12 foot rooms are beside the larger main kennel area. One is her whelping room, filled with the rabbit hutches. The other is her office & sick room. Sick animals should not be kept in the same room as young pups and healthy dogs. By having a separate room for the office, prospective buyers see only the dogs she personally wants them to see or sell. By keeping them from seeing the entire lot of dogs, they were prevented from "falling in love" with the dog or pup she had intended to keep, or one already sold. The possibility of future theft also was curtailed. A Rottweiler pup, raised with her Poms, provides additional security. "She watches the kennel for me when I have to be away for short periods during the day", says Debbie.

An 8 foot high privacy fence was constructed around the kennel to keep the dogs in, people out, and cut down on the barking caused by the dogs being able to see everything that moves around them. Debbie is a firm believer, that, even if you live out in the country, you have a duty to not let your dogs bark and disturb your neighbors.

The dogs are corrected when they bark. If she raises them from puppies, they are trained with a squirt bottle of water. If they bark, she squirts. A radio left playing in the kennel also keeps the dogs quiet.

Should everything else fail at keeping a dog quiet when necessary, they are "debarked" by the vet, a procedure done while they are under anesthesia, and causes them little pain, if any, afterwards. The result is a happier dog since he is not scolded for his stubborn habit anymore. The "whisper" bark which results after the surgery, lets the previously noisy dog continue his habit..only in a wonderfully quiet way!

Kennel Ideas

Kenneth M. Lewis
Newberg, Oregon — Zoologist

Mr. Lewis, now retired, was a Ken-L-Biskit salesman for 25 years, a zoologist and experimental biologist and museum director before that. His experience with caging animals therefore is immense. He has seen hundreds of kennels, none of which were anywhere near perfect, but many had at least one idea that he latched onto.

Sawdust was found to be the best material for a kennel run according to Mr. Lewis. To dispose of the droppings, a compost heap was used. A long fenced area was constructed with aluminum siding on the surface of the ground. There were no flies, no odor, no plugged sewer drains to contend with and best of all, lots of fertilizer not going to waste.

His three compost pens are each about 5 feet wide and 10 feet long, with iron reinforcing bars used to keep the aluminum sheets vertical. Into the first pen, dog droppings, sawdust that has been cleaned out of the runs, kitchen garbage, grass clippings, weeds and horse or cow manure from a neighbors barn, are thrown. Any exposed droppings are covered with a shovel full of sawdust to keep away flies and control odor. Lime and additional fertilizer are added and the compost kept quite wet by hosing down with water, when necessary. When the bin is full, he plants a cover crop of grass seed and clover. He then starts a second bin, and when it is partially filled, takes some from the first bin and mixes it into the second bin.

By this time, the first bin is loaded with earth worms, which have helped break down the compost. The natural heat generated by fungus action, contributes further.

It helps, if you can, to make a layer of droppings and garbage, then a layer of dirt or soil. He keeps three bins going and the rich black soil that comes out is excellent for the garden or shrubs. "Just don't tell your dinner guest the vegetables have been fertilized with dog droppings", he says humorously! Seriously though, it's a great way, he says, to keep down your sewer bills and a heck of a lot easier than controlling the smell of urine from a cement run.

One of the best fencing materials is a 1 inch square welded mesh wire. It is 4 feet high and comes in 100 foot rolls. It is galvanized after welding, so it will resist rust for many years. A dog cannot get his nose, tail, ears or paws through it. It is hard to climb and hard for a dog to get his teeth into. Stapled to a 2x4 inch wood frame, it can be easily replaced when necessary, and does not require special tools to do so.

Do not use cedar shavings or cedar sawdust without testing to see if you or your dogs are allergic to cedar. It can cause an asthma-like condition and severe rash upon contact, or a digestive upset upon ingestion.

For solid inside walls, where dogs can come into contact with them, 1/8 inch cement board is an excellent material. It is brittle, however, so it should have plenty of backing when putting up.

Other materials he prefers are Formica, oil tempered masonite and the new seamless materials such as fiberglass, torquinol, capri and epoxy resin paints. Consult your local paint and lumber yard for the latest developments.

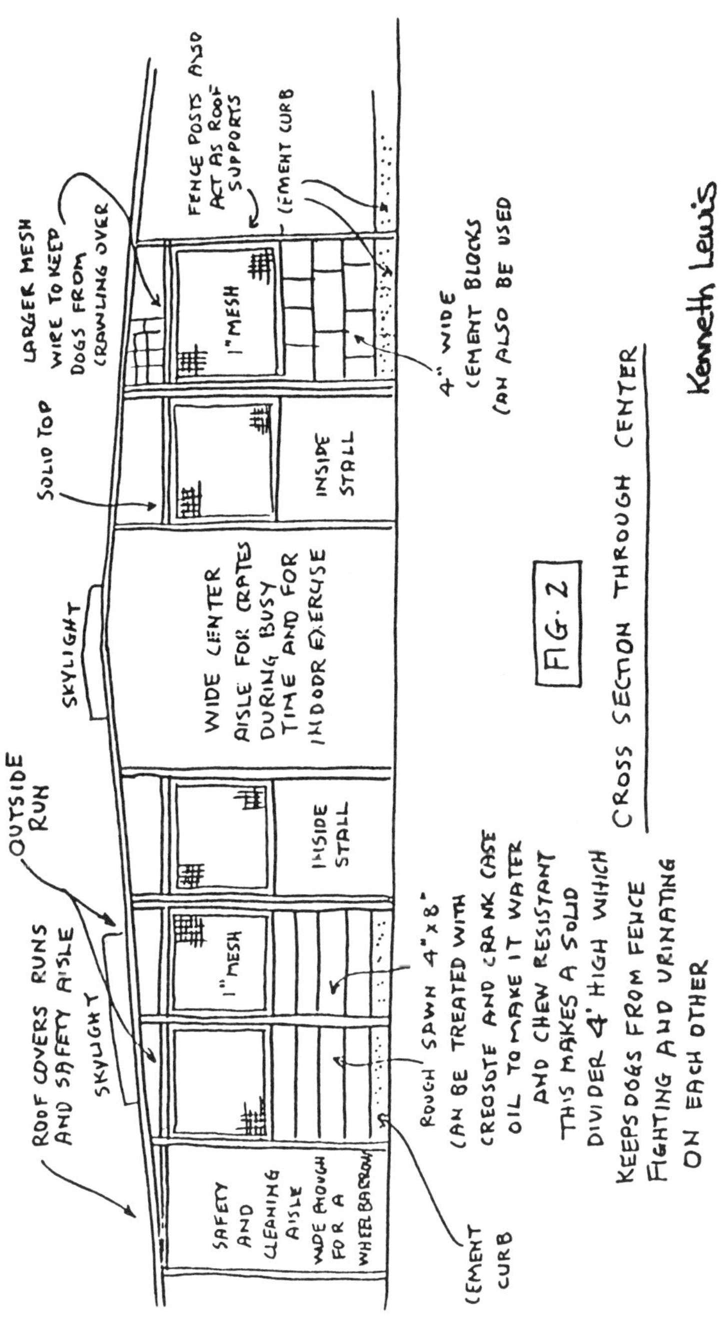
ROOF COVERS RUNS AND SAFETY AISLE
OUTSIDE RUN
SKYLIGHT
SKYLIGHT
SOLID TOP
LARGER MESH WIRE TO KEEP DOGS FROM CRAWLING OVER
FENCE POSTS ALSO ACT AS ROOF SUPPORTS
CEMENT CURB
1" MESH
4" WIDE CEMENT BLOCKS CAN ALSO BE USED
INSIDE STALL
WIDE CENTER AISLE FOR CRATES DURING BUSY TIME AND FOR INDOOR EXERCISE
INSIDE STALL
1" MESH
SAFETY AND CLEANING AISLE WIDE ENOUGH FOR A WHEELBARROW
CEMENT CURB
ROUGH SAWN 4"x8" CAN BE TREATED WITH CREOSOTE AND CRANK CASE OIL TO MAKE IT WATER AND CHEW RESISTANT THIS MAKES A SOLID DIVIDER 4' HIGH WHICH KEEPS DOGS FROM FENCE FIGHTING AND URINATING ON EACH OTHER
FIG. 2
CROSS SECTION THROUGH CENTER
Kenneth Lewis

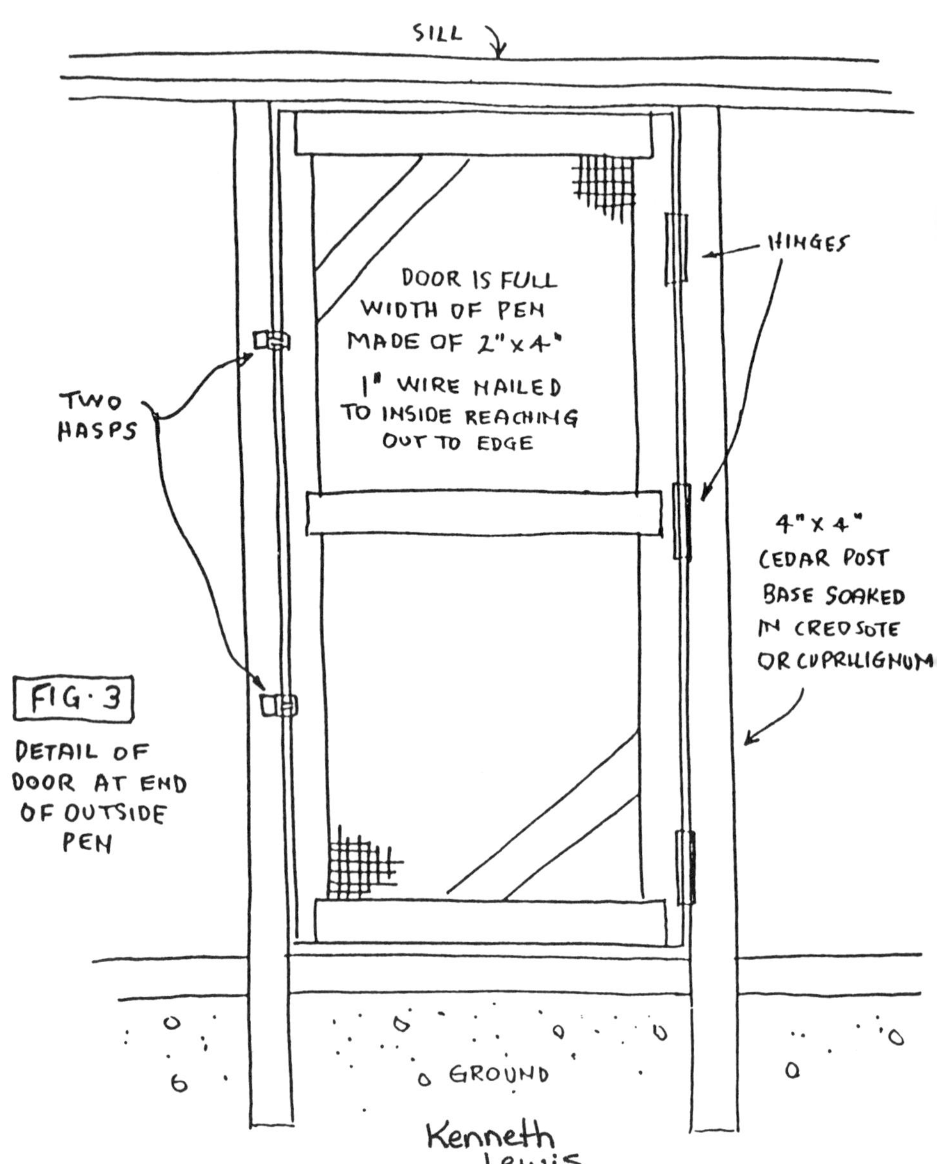
SILL
HINGES
DOOR IS FULL
WIDTH OF PEN
MADE OF 2"x4"
1" WIRE NAILED
TO INSIDE REACHING
OUT TO EDGE
TWO
HASPS
4"x4"
CEDAR POST
BASE SOAKED
IN CREOSOTE
OR CUPRILIGNUM
FIG·3
DETAIL OF
DOOR AT END
OF OUTSIDE
PEN
GROUND
Kenneth
Lewis

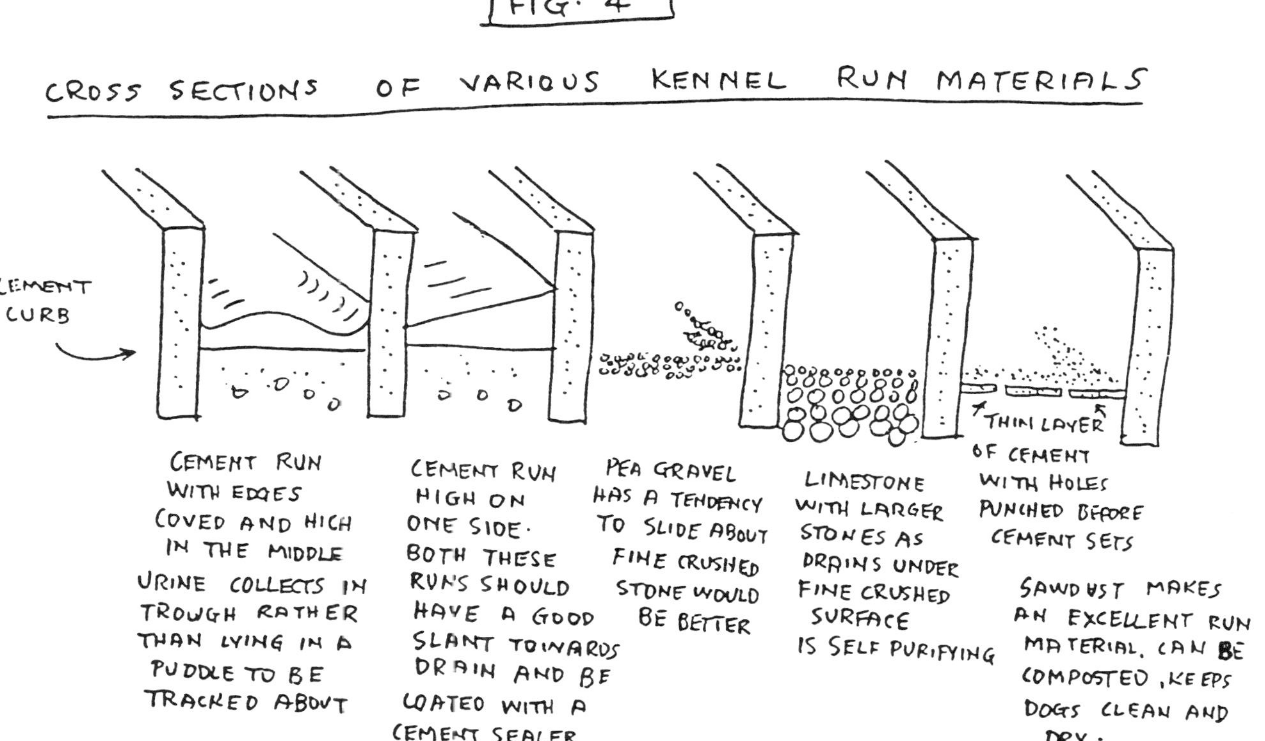
FIG. 4
CROSS SECTIONS OF VARIOUS KENNEL RUN MATERIALS
CEMENT CURB
CEMENT RUN WITH EDGES COVED AND HIGH IN THE MIDDLE
URINE COLLECTS IN TROUGH RATHER THAN LYING IN A PUDDLE TO BE TRACKED ABOUT
CEMENT RUN HIGH ON ONE SIDE.
BOTH THESE RUNS SHOULD HAVE A GOOD SLANT TOWARDS DRAIN AND BE COATED WITH A CEMENT SEALER
PEA GRAVEL HAS A TENDENCY TO SLIDE ABOUT FINE CRUSHED STONE WOULD BE BETTER
LIMESTONE WITH LARGER STONES AS DRAINS UNDER FINE CRUSHED SURFACE IS SELF PURIFYING
THIN LAYER OF CEMENT WITH HOLES PUNCHED BEFORE CEMENT SETS
SAWDUST MAKES AN EXCELLENT RUN MATERIAL, CAN BE COMPOSTED, KEEPS DOGS CLEAN AND DRY.
Kenneth Lewis

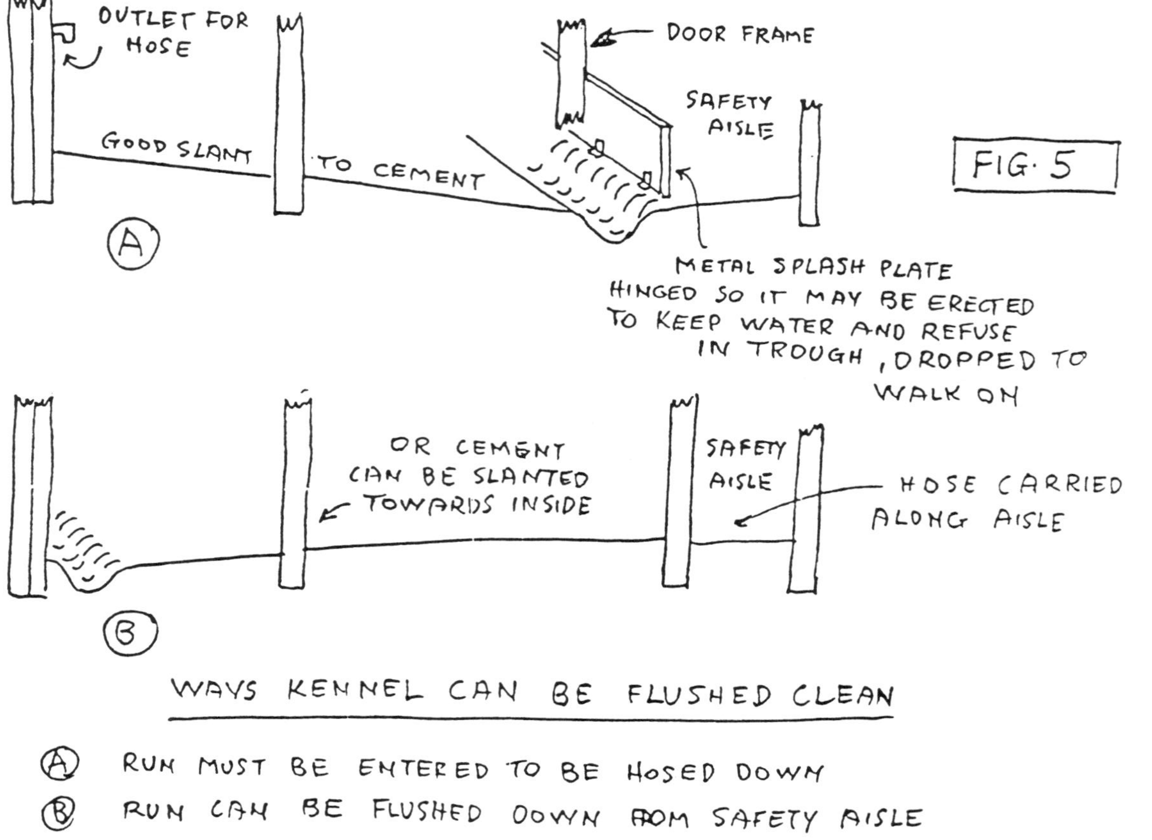
OUTLET FOR HOSE
DOOR FRAME
SAFETY AISLE
GOOD SLANT
TO CEMENT
FIG. 5
A
METAL SPLASH PLATE HINGED SO IT MAY BE ERECTED TO KEEP WATER AND REFUSE IN TROUGH, DROPPED TO WALK ON
OR CEMENT CAN BE SLANTED TOWARDS INSIDE
SAFETY AISLE
HOSE CARRIED ALONG AISLE
B
WAYS KENNEL CAN BE FLUSHED CLEAN
(A) RUN MUST BE ENTERED TO BE HOSED DOWN
(B) RUN CAN BE FLUSHED DOWN FROM SAFETY AISLE

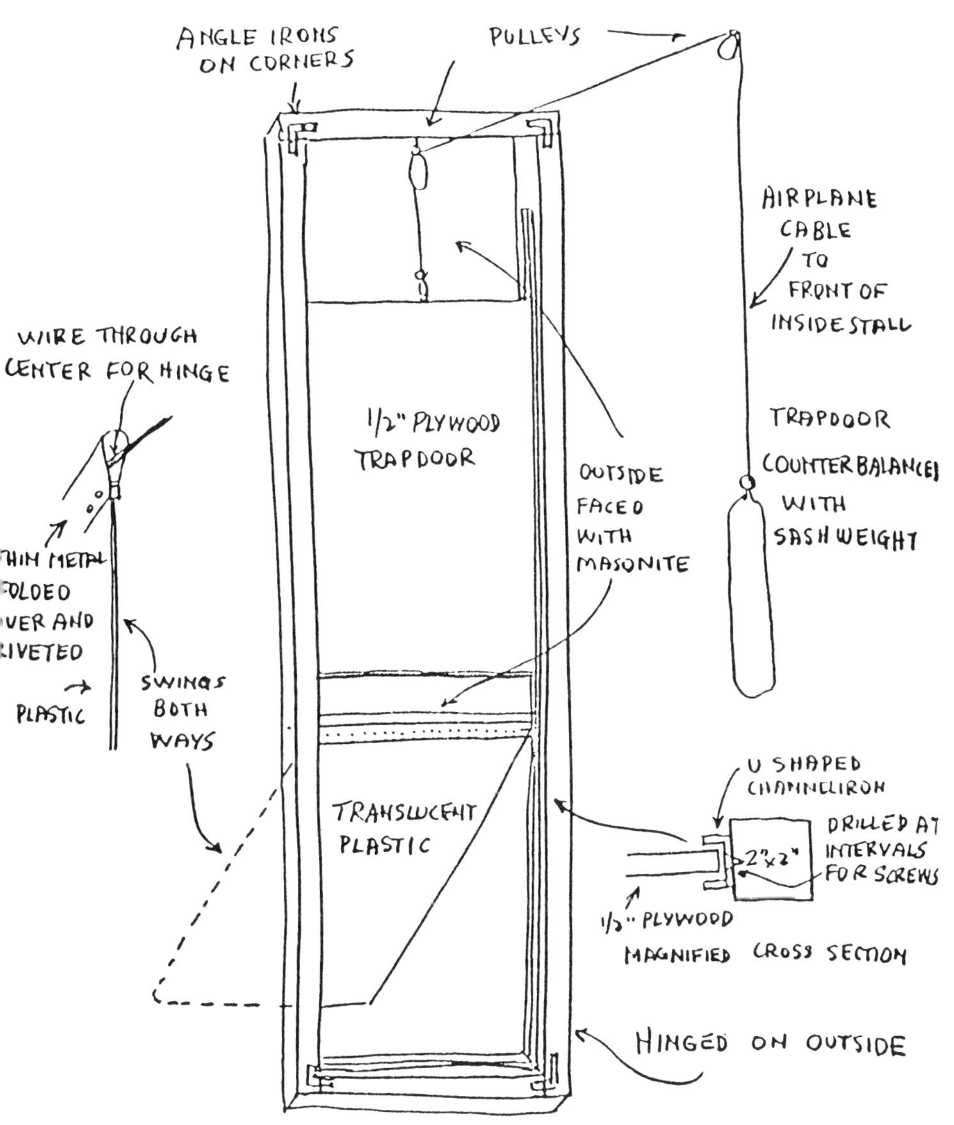

DETAIL OF TRAPDOOR IN A DOOR TO OUTSIDE RUN

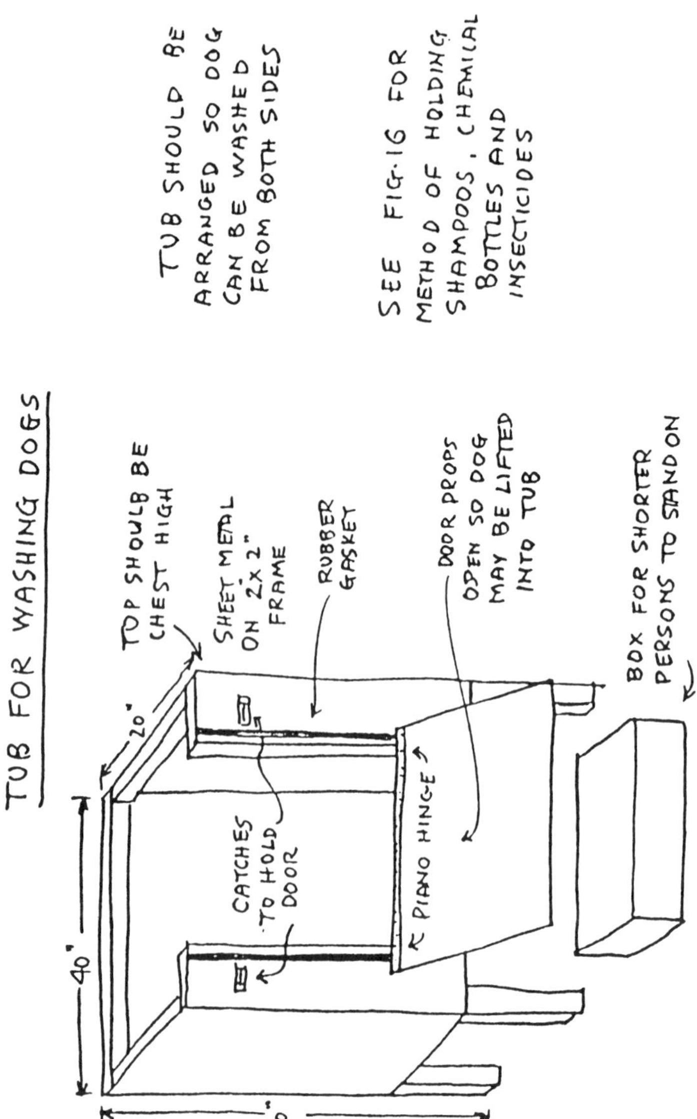
TUB FOR WASHING DOGS
TOP SHOULB BE CHEST HIGH
SHEET METAL ON 2"X 2" FRAME
RUBBER GASKET
DOOR PROPS OPEN SO DOG MAY BE LIFTED INTO TUB
BOX FOR SHORTER PERSONS TO STAND ON
CATCHES TO HOLD DOOR
PIANO HINGE
20"
40"
60"
TUB SHOULD BE ARRANGED SO DOG CAN BE WASHED FROM BOTH SIDES
SEE FIG-16 FOR METHOD OF HOLDING SHAMPOOS, CHEMICAL BOTTLES AND INSECTICIDES

IN AND OUT CRATES

IN A BOARDING KENNEL IT IS A GOOD IDEA TO HAVE "IN" AND "OUT" CRATES TO PUT DOGS IN WHILE OWNERS ARE GIVING INFORMATION OR SETTLING ACCOUNTS. CRATES ARE IN THE OFFICE WALL, DOUBLE-ENDED SO DOGS CAN BE PUT IN OR TAKEN OUT EITHER END.

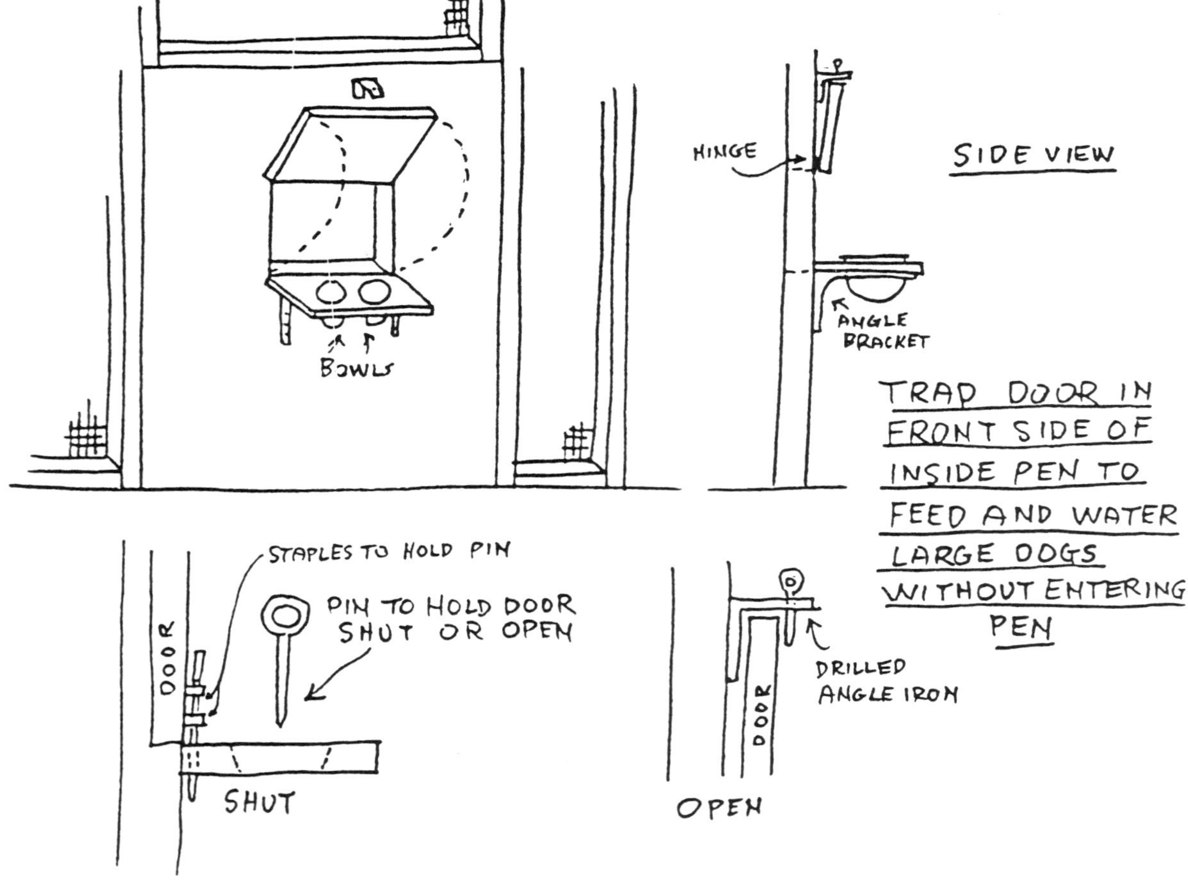
BOWLS
HINGE
SIDE VIEW
ANGLE BRACKET
TRAP DOOR IN FRONT SIDE OF INSIDE PEN TO FEED AND WATER LARGE DOGS WITHOUT ENTERING PEN
STAPLES TO HOLD PIN
PIN TO HOLD DOOR SHUT OR OPEN
DOOR
SHUT
DRILLED ANGLE IRON
DOOR
OPEN

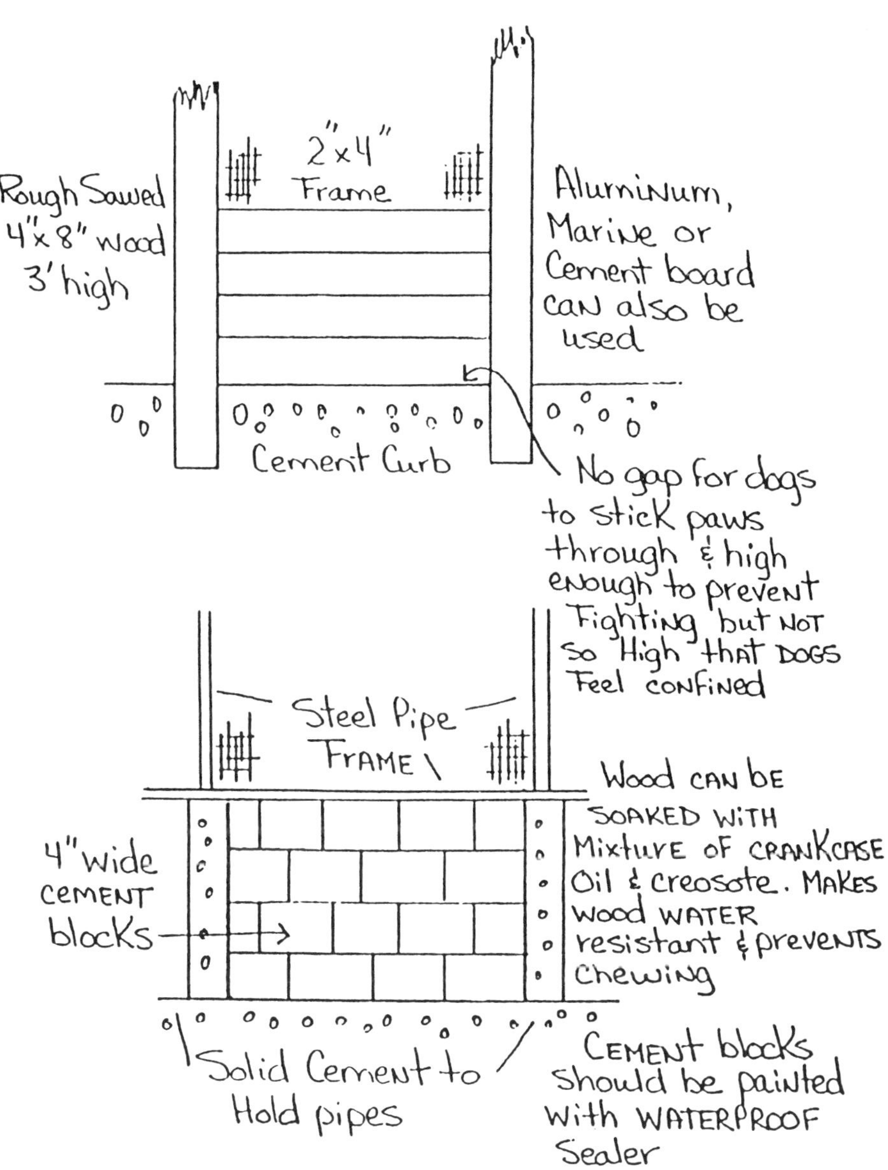

DIVIDERS BETWEEN OUTSIDE RUNS

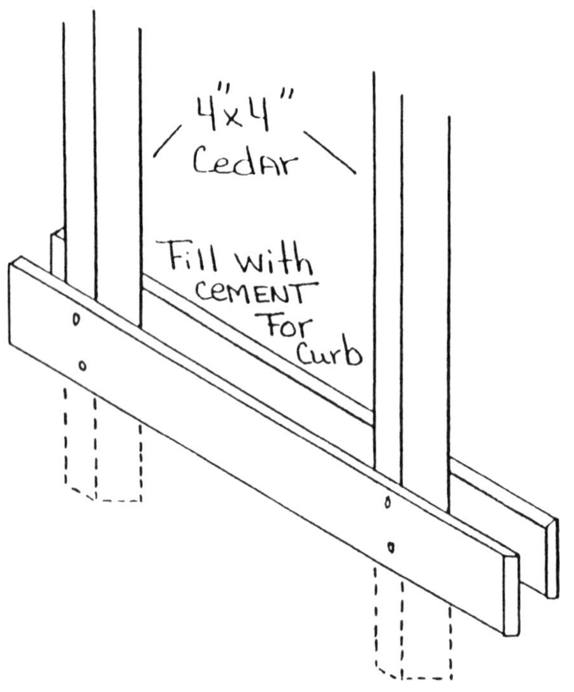
4"x4"
Cedar
Fill with
CEMENT
For
Curb

Mrs. Margaret John
Marvale Silky Terriers
Romoland, California

Silky Terriers

For those who prefer a kennel adjoining the house, Mrs. John sent in an extra nice plan.

At the time they had their house built, they also had the builder add on the following to the end of the house. The addition, which measures approximately 10x20 feet cost approximately $2,500 and contains:

- Laundry Tub
- Concrete Floor with floor drain
- 3 sliding windows
- Insulation in 2 exterior walls & ceiling
- Electrical outlets
- 2 - 6 foot luminous light fixtures
- Water-proof Formica sheets on 3 walls 2 feet high so room could be hosed down
- Window-mounted air conditioner/heater with thermostat control

Another $1,650 was spent on the extras below:

Custom-made built-in cabinets with 4 drawers	$350
4 Shur-Loc runs 3x12 feet	$565
4 Johnson Pet Doors	$81
Outside Roof covering	$350
Screen Door	$90
Small gravel for runs	$40
Intercom in bedroom	$99
Telephone Extension	$25

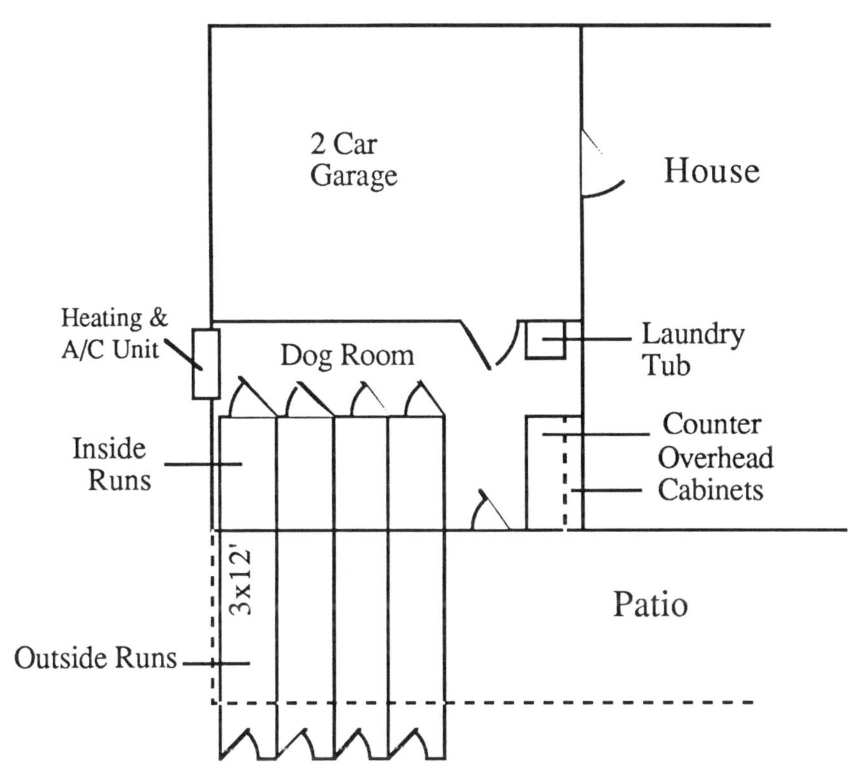
2 Car
Garage
House
Heating &
A/C Unit
Dog Room
Laundry
Tub
Counter
Overhead
Cabinets
Inside
Runs
3x12'
Patio
Outside Runs

Kibble is kept in a 30 gallon trash can. For disposing of wastes she uses a 5 gallon plastic bucket with a lid and a plastic bag inserted inside. When full, she just ties the bag and disposes of it in the trash. Works great for toy dogs!

Crates can be stacked nicely under the counter. The dogs sleep in their crates at night. Airline crates are stacked against the wall opposite the inside runs.

The kennel has four exercise pens that are used on the patio when the weather outside is nice, and set up indoors when needed for pups. The dogs can come from their room through the garage (which is kept closed) into the kitchen and family room, without fear of them getting loose. They take turns in the house, since there are 5 or more of them.

The back yard is approximately 10,000 square feet, fenced 6 feet high to protect from stray dogs, people and sometimes coyotes. The dogs take turns running in the yard, a couple at a time.

The Johns live about 2 to 3 miles from Sun City, California, 30 miles south of Riverside. The temperatures reach as high as 110 degrees in the summer and 30 degrees in the winter. With temperatures controlled thermostatically, she is able to leave all day, when needed, and knows that the dogs are not too cold or too hot, and that they are safe.

Mrs. John has had Silky Terriers since 1969 and has made champions of 8 males and 1 female. When she first moved to this location, she obtained a private kennel license from Riverdale County which allowed her to have as many dogs as she wanted. The animal control officer who came out to inspect before issuing the license, was so excited about her setup that he brought the Chief control officer back to see it. They said it was such a pleasure to see a kennel so complete and sanitary!

Kennel Ideas

Cheryl L. Anderson
Aberdeen Acres
Stephenson, Virginia

Cheryl's kennel building is 92 feet long and 30 feet wide. The walls are 8 feet high and are constructed of solid, poured concrete, as well as the floors. The actual kennel area is 80x30 feet and the remaining 30x12 feet is for a work area. The inside runs are 4x12 feet for small dogs and 6x12 feet for larger ones. The runs have a 4 foot solid panel between them and then chain link fencing the remaining 2 feet to make the partitions 6 feet high.

Each run has a dog door that is 29 inches high and 17 inches wide that slides up and down. This allows her to decide who comes and goes, and when. The door leads outside to an equally wide, but 14 foot long concrete run. There is just plain 6 foot high chain link fencing on the outside runs. Two large exercise areas are fenced outside.

In the work area there is a tub and dipping area, a stove and refrigerator and a room for food storage. The work area is attached to another building which shares the common office and waiting room. This area connects on to an eight stall barn. The two buildings that connect form an "L" shaped offset.

A small portion of the work area is set aside for whelping facilities as well as one of the inside runs.

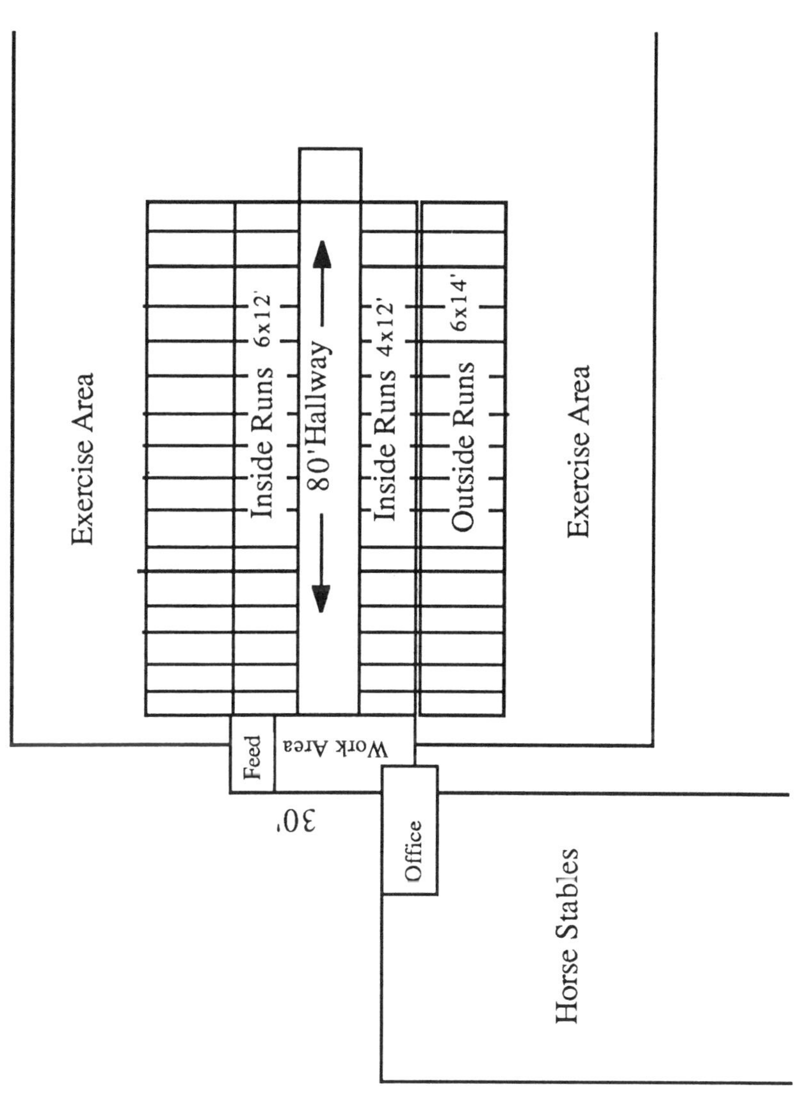
Exercise Area
Inside Runs 6x12'
80'Hallway
Inside Runs 4x12'
Outside Runs 6x14'
Exercise Area
Feed
Work Area
30'
Office
Horse Stables

Heat for the building is provided by a large wood stove. The smaller runs are located closest to the end where the wood stove is. This will allow the small dogs that need the heat to be nearer to it, and the larger dogs, who need it less, at the other end of the building.

Dog waste is handled by a septic system. The middle of the concrete floor slopes off to each side, so that any water in the aisle will run into a run area. This will flow into a drain that runs along the back of each run and slopes down to the far end so that it can empty into the septic system. The outside runs are also sloped so that the wastes run down and off to one side into the system.

Mason fencing is used with swinging gates inside and outside. Feed and water bowls in each kennel are attached so that feeding can be done without having to enter the kennel.

A power nozzle that hooks onto a garden hose gives about 125 pounds of water pressure to cut down on cleaning time and water consumption.

Estimated costs to build her kennel run about $40,000 with an additional $15,000 for fencing.

Blain Kukevitch	Miniature Schnauzers
Stone Oak Kennel	Doberman Pinchers
Plainfield, Connecticut	Shar-Pei

Plainfield is a little town on the East Coast about one hour northeast of Hartford, Connecticut. Blain built and designed his own kennel as a hobby, with intentions of one day devoting full time to it, having already finished his first Champion Shar-Pei. The kennel is nicely set up and lots of people have complemented him on the design he says.

The kennel is 12x32 feet. The first building was only 12x16 feet and was added onto after discovering that it was not large enough. To enlarge, he simply added the same dimensions to one side, doubling his original building.

Along the back wall there are seven pens that measure 4x4 feet. These can be used for either breeding, whelping or storage when not in use otherwise. This pen also has a full sized door in the back for a fire escape.

On the front side is a sink and countertop that measures 3x8 feet. Also on the front side of the building are a total of eight pens that measure 1 1/2 x 4 feet with removable divider boards to make the pens larger when needed. The pens are 24 inches high and are just right for the breeds he raises.

The 4x4 foot pens, on the back of the kennel, have doors that lead outside to 4x10 foot runs. They all have gates that open up to a 50x60 foot sand run on the end of the building. This is where the pups are exercised. Four holding crates are in this area just in case the dogs need to be separated.

All of the flooring is cement and all of the walls, either plywood or sheet rock. There are plenty of windows to allow light and fresh air in. A Kerosene heater and electric heat keep the building warm in cold weather. The building has both hot and cold running water, with the water heater installed under the counter.

Above the first 12x16 foot part of the building is a loft that measures 12x8 feet, that he uses for storage.

Four, 4-foot florescent lights are hung down the middle of the kennel indoors and plenty of outlets were installed to plug in heat lamps, clippers, etc.

The total building, according to Blain, could be built with everything included, for around $10,000.

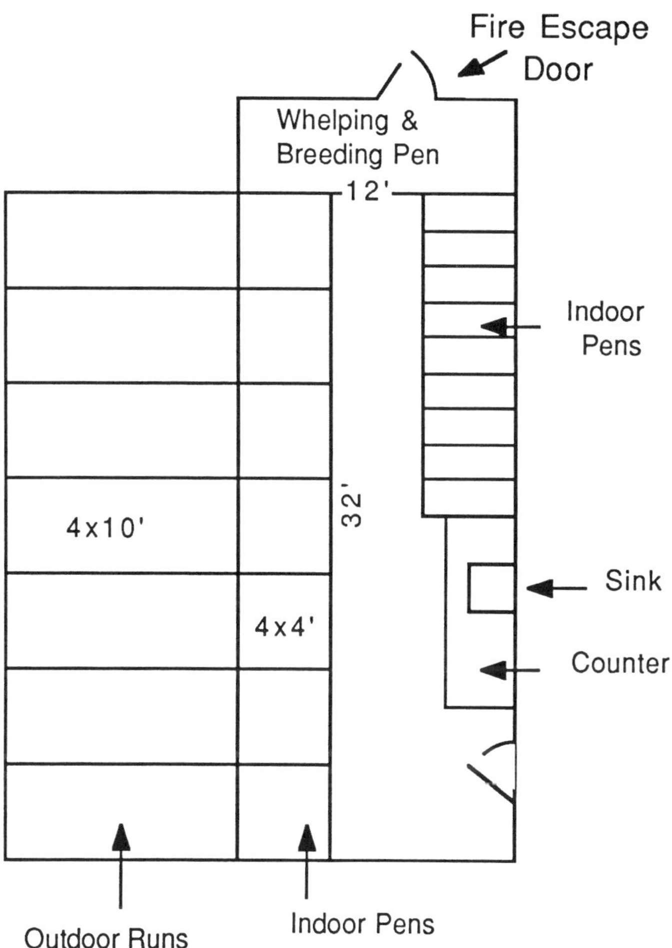
Fire Escape
Door
Whelping &
Breeding Pen
12'
Indoor
Pens
32'
4x10'
Sink
4x4'
Counter
Outdoor Runs
Indoor Pens

Kennel Ideas

Letty Larson Afong
Neocles Kennels
St. Paul, Minnesota

Standard Poodles
West Highland Whites

Lettie submitted a rough draft of her current kennel, the fourth one she's built in 22 years. She says it's a very practical one.

Features

Runs are covered to protect dogs from the sun

Privacy fence on outside

Kennel room is heated & insulated

Dogs can be brought into the house through the garage

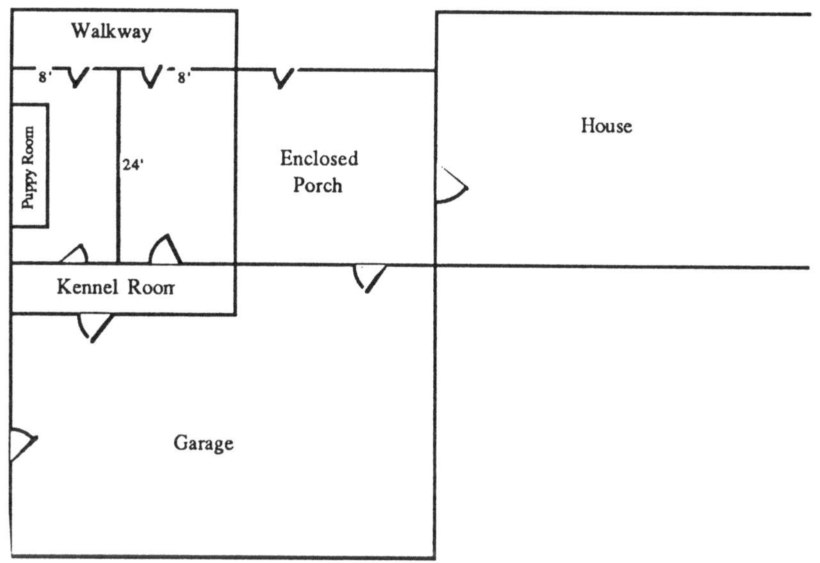
Walkway
8'
8'
Puppy Room
24'
Enclosed
Porch
House
Kennel Room
Garage

Julia Chalmers
Iowa City, Iowa — Standard Schnauzers

When exposed to hot temperatures, young puppies can't pant, so the heat really affects them.

Wet a towel and place them on it. Even three day old pups will crawl to it after putting them on it only once.

This idea is also good for dogs of any age, in the heat, especially older ones in poor health. They lie on the towel and go to sleep. Once accustomed to this pleasure, they can't seem to do without it.

Jim & Kathy Corbett
Aloha, Oregon — Black & Tan Coonhounds

In our large breed, protecting puppies from accidental "squashing" is always a concern. Instead of a whelping box, we use a large wading pool.

It is soft enough that there is some "give" between mother and pups and it is very easy to take outside and hose out for cleaning.

These pools can be purchased quite reasonably at the end of summer...another advantage!

Kathy Gabbert
Dickinson, North Dakota

Standard Poodles

I have very good luck feeding "Lamb milk replacer" to puppies who are 3 to 9 weeks in age.

It is higher in fat & protein than calf milk replacer and comes in powdered, 25 pound bags, making it very economical to feed.

They get plenty of fresh water, Purina Beef Flavored Puppy Chow and turn out to be happy, healthy pups!

Kennel Ideas

Ron & Jane Meyer
Stormy Farm Samoyeds
Storm Lake, Iowa

Samoyeds

The Meyers have come up with an overhead panel in the runs to keep dogs from standing up on their back legs.

The panels are used mainly on puppy runs until they are about 2 years old. This prevents the dog from putting all of his weight on his rear legs while his bone structure is not yet full strength.

The support for the overhead panels is provided by 2 inch angle iron strips. These run the length of the run on both sides, approximately 48 inches above the cement floor, and have a lip at the gate end to keep it in place. By making the wire overhead panels 22 inches shorter than the length of the run, the wire panel can be pushed to the other end when you wish to open the door into the kennel.

Cement dishes, available from a local cement factory, are used for watering to prevent the dogs from dumping them over.

Vicki Haase Hill
Hill St. OES
Colorado Springs
Colorado

Old English Sheep dogs

As a breeder of Old English Sheep dogs, and having just had a litter within the past few days, the ideas I have relate to breeding & whelping.

One problem I have had in the past is weighing newborns. If they are healthy, normal puppies, they wiggle and squirm when they are put on the scale, and it is hard to get an accurate weight (which is important to know from day to day to make sure they are gaining weight and flourishing).

The solution to this problem came during the last litter. The dam contracted metritis and had to consume quite a few antibiotics. The vet told me to make sure the puppies received some plain, low fat yogurt every day in order to keep the flora and fauna at the right levels in their stomachs. By accident, I put a small dab of yogurt on the puppies tongues right before I weighed them. Voila! The puppy was so busy tasting and smacking his lips that he "forgot" to squirm so much and I got a much more accurate weight.

Also, in the summer heat (especially with heavily coated breeds such as mine) during the whelping and afterwards, my girls will take a little cool nourishment. I buy cans of plain chicken broth and refrigerate it till needed. It's always appreciated by my girls, since whelping areas need to be warm and free from drafts.

Kennel Ideas

Judy L. Secaur
Fantasia Basenjis
Coeur d'Alene, Idaho

Basenjis

For my first temporary kennel I didn't want the expense or permanency of concrete, so I used patio blocks, starting with about the first 3 or 4 feet. I added some each time I found them on sale.

I started by adding a 10x22 foot room to the back of our garage. It has three, 4x6 foot windows, to take advantage of the southern exposure. There are four indoor runs approximately 4x5 feet and one indoor run approximately 5x10 feet for pups. All have doors leading to 24 foot outdoor runs. All runs are double fenced with welded wire. Each has a little house about the size of a #200 crate. Carpet samples are used on top and inside of them for the dogs to lie on. These last for 3 or 4 washings.

Two 30x60 foot grassed pens provide exercise and loafing areas for summer use. A large tarp over the runs provides shade and keeps the indoors & outdoors cool.

Top hanging pet doors did not work well for Basenjis. They tend to rub their tail hair off and give them bald spots on the top of their tails. Side opening doors cured the problem.

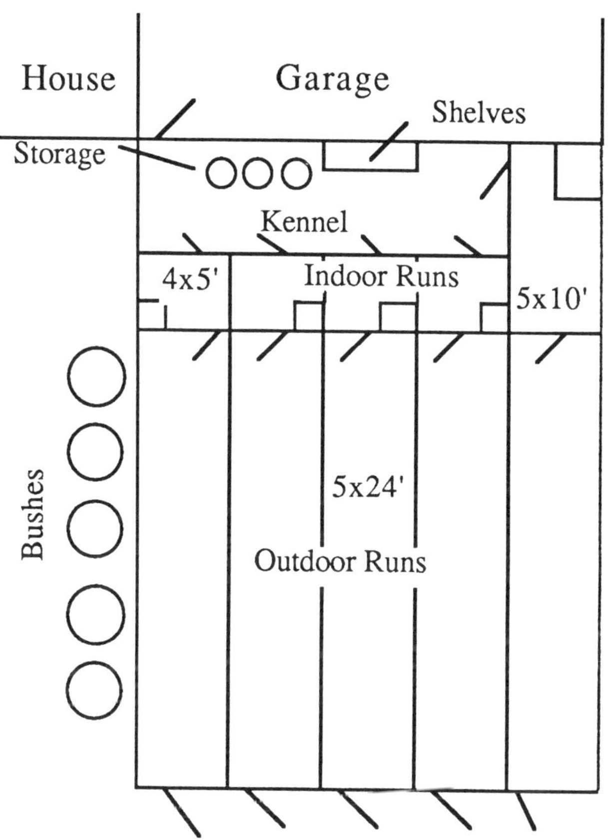
House
Garage
Shelves
Storage
Kennel
4x5'
Indoor Runs
5x10'
Bushes
5x24'
Outdoor Runs

In the house I found it necessary to keep the dogs in or out of certain areas and still have good air circulation. Our family room door was cut in half and turned into a Dutch door. By closing the bottom half, we still have good air and keep the dogs in or out.

In the upstairs hall, I made a gate with a section of white, vinyl coated child and puppy pen fence purchased from a Sears Catalog and 4 eye bolts. I mounted 2 eye bolts on each wall, then ran one of the rods through the eye bolts and rod just short enough that the hook at the top would drop through an eye bolt at the top as the rod was dropped into the eye bolt at the bottom. I don't have to climb over it, as you do so many gates, and I can open up the rooms for fresh air without fear of the dogs making a mess or chewing something up. To go through, I simply lift the rod up out of the eye bolts about 3 inches.

Louise H. Strickland
Lou's Toy Manchester Terriers
Spring Hope, North Carolina

Toy Manchester Terriers

I raise Toy Manchester Terriers the easy way in a heavy cardboard box with a door cut out and lined with a bath mat.

The bed box is placed inside an 8x10 foot wire cage. The wire floor is off of the cement flooring and is layered with newspapers. All food and water for the bitch and later, the puppies, is kept outside the bed box. Pups are easily trained to use the paper when they get old enough to get out of the bed box.

They first start eating or nibbling their mothers' food, then have their own food and water in low containers. The puppies learn quickly to eat and to eliminate waste before going back into the bed box just like the mother does. Soiled paper is replaced with clean newspapers and the bedding bath mat is changed as needed and washed.

In the winter I raise puppies in the bathroom in a pasteboard box on a bath mat. If the weather is cold, I use a large covered heating pad for the very young pups. The cord goes through a corner hole in the box.

As the puppies get old enough to want more space, I attach another larger, paper-lined box with a cut-out door. The soiled paper is replaced with clean newspaper and the bedding and heating pad covers are changed as needed.

When the puppies get large enough to start jumping out of the boxes, I substitute taller boxes.

There is little or no expense involved since cardboard boxes and newspapers are so plentiful. Bath mats and extra covers (homemade) for heating pads can be washed regularly.

All Natual flea control

Diatomaceous Earth

Diatomaceous Earth is a natural, non-chemical product. It appears to be a powder, but it is actually razor-sharp crystals to fleas. It blocks and cuts the fleas' gills and they die.

You can find cans of it at your local garden shop or building supply stores such as Home Depot or Lowes. Simply sprinkle in carpets and around crevices.

Kay Cox
Countrylane Kennels
Pike Road, Alabama

Pembroke Welsh Corgis

Our kennel yard has several trees which, here in Alabama, attract hundreds of birds every spring. This has been an aggravating problem with the birds eating and drinking from dog dishes and depositing their droppings everywhere. This spring, at our local hardware store, I bought two "scarecrows". One is a life-sized owl, the other a 5 foot snake. Both are inflatable and very life-like. I also bought three garden black cats, with marble eyes, from a gift catalog. I placed the inflatables on the lower branches of trees around the yard. The results were amazing. The birds would hover over the trees and then suddenly disappear. This was a simple solution to a big problem. You do need to keep moving the "scarecrows" around to keep the birds fooled, however.

Here in Alabama it is terribly hot, and some of our pens don't have enough shade. What we do is transplant every easy growing tree we can find on our farm and place them around or even inside of the runs. The best results we have had, in this area, are popcorn and willow trees. These grow so fast that it is unbelievable. The willows need lots of water in the summer, however. Each year we also buy a live evergreen Christmas tree and plant it after Christmas around the kennel area.

To combat the flea problem in the runs and yard, I sprinkle Rough Salt (it comes in 25 pound bags at the grocery store) lightly everywhere. Too much will kill the grass. Dogs are taken out of the runs prior to treating them with salt. Once the gravel is spread with salt, it is misted down with a hose. Fleas, as well as ants are killed. Since I do not like to use strong chemicals around my kennel, this method is great!

A product called "Critter Carpet"sold by Show Quality Pet Products of Hopkins, Minnesota, is great for whelping pens, to line crates and even works for bedding in dog houses and kennel buildings. It stays dry because moisture goes through it. It gets softer with each washing. Another plus..I have used it with 24 permanent Corgis and numerous new litters and it is absolutely "chew proof". (At least with my breed). The carpet can be purchased in pieces, or more cheaply, by the yard. All you have to do is cut it in the various sizes you need.

A small child's play pool made of plastic makes the best whelping box ever. I line it with newspaper and then put "Critter Carpet" on top of it. I also put an exercise pen around the entire pool when I need to keep the mother confined in a small space. She can easily come and go into the box at will. It is easily cleaned with a very mild disinfectant and great when you must travel with a new litter since it easily sets up in motel rooms.

Dot Wallace
Horse Shoe Kennels
Old Ocean, Texas Hestsko Norwegian Elkhounds

As breeders of a Northern breed in a hot, humid climate, I have happened upon a good remedy for "hot" spotson my dogs.

After a very long, wet spell this past spring, one of my puppies suddenly developed a very large, moist, painful "hot" spot under her tail. I had just sent in entries on her in puppy class in some upcoming shows. To pull her would break the majors, so in desperation I tried something new.

Since most "hot" spots are very moist and all the remedies the vet had given me were also moist, apparently burned when applied and were a horrible color that stained the surrounding coat, I decided to look around for a better solution. I happened to have a bottle of antibiotic ear powder, the kind bought for routine grooming without a prescription. I thought "why not?" It's antibiotic and white, so it won't stain the coat.

The spot dried up overnight and the exudate was easily brushed from the surrounding undercoat leaving a clean, healthy area for the new hair to grow in. With the powder there is no need to shave or clip any of the coat as it will penetrate the dense coat surrounding the spot and prevent its spread.

I have since used the remedy with equally good results. The pup in question won a major that weekend at 6 months of age even though the hair had not completely grown back in!

Suggested Emergency First Aid Kit

Can of dog food

bottle of hydrogen peroxide - 3% solution

turkey baster or bulb syringe

saline eye solution fo flush out contaminants

artificial tear gel to lubricate eyes after flushing

mild grease-cutting dishwashing detergent to bathe animal after skin contamination

rubber gloves to prevent handler's exposure

forceps to remove stingers

muzzle to keep animal from hurting handler

pet carrier to transport to vet

Miriam Smith
Middleton, Ohio Beagles

Since we don't have a great deal of yard around our kennel the problem with dog droppings was solved by composting them in 5 to 7 gallon plastic buckets that restaurants frequently throw away. They have a wire handle and tight-fitting lids and are sturdy enough when full.

We drill about 6 to 9 holes around the sides of the buckets (about 1/2 diameter holes) spacing them evenly both around and from top to bottom and a few in the bottom of the bucket.

We start by putting a couple of inches of wood ashes in the bottom of the bucket. We then add a day's worth of droppings and often incorporate kitchen scraps as well. We immediately cover this layer with a layer of dirt and repeat the process the next day adding moisture to keep it damp but not soggy. When the bucket is nearly full we set it aside and start another bucket. To encourage decomposition we agitate the full buckets often so that everything will mix together. In warm weather it only takes about 3 to 5 weeks to complete the process of decomposition.

When ready, we shovel this rich humus around plants in the yard.

Kennel Ideas

Mandy Smith
Lotus Point Shar-Pei
Folsom, New Jersey 08037 Shar-Pei

We all know how expensive dog beds can be, particularly those orthopedic ones. Well, I bought one of those therapeutic mattress pads for a twin size bed for $6.97. It is the same stuff they use for the orthopedic dog beds.

I cut it across the width into 3 pieces. Each piece was 24 inches by 36 inches. I then covered each piece with a blanket I use for dogs (or you can use sheets) and folded the excess blanket under the pad.

Now you can place them in dog crates or on the floor inside the house. I got 3 beds for a fraction of the cost of one!

What I really like best is that they cut very easily with regular scissors and you can take the blanket off to wash them. You can also cut these into different sizes to suit the needs of your breed.

For small breeds you can cut them down and stuff them into old pillow cases. Imagine how many beds you can make from a king-size mattress pad. I have 7 dogs and this saves me a good deal of money on dog beds and gives my dogs great comfort.

The only problem I can think of is if someone has a destructive dog who may tear these beds apart. My Chinese Shar-Pei are not destructive so I have not run into this problem.

Sharon Woloshen
Chilcote Reg. Kennels
Chomedey, Laval
Quebec, Canada

Siberian Huskies

While I was constructing my outdoor runs I found 3/4 inch gravel worked well for drainage, but when it came time to lay the cement patio blocks it would have been impossible to level and grade on top of such large gravel. I consulted a renovation center and I was told to use rock dust. Another place however told me that rock dust, when wet, would turn into cement, and there would go my drainage. I therefore used 1/4 inch gravel on top of the 3/4 inch gravel bed It worked fine and the drainage is still all that I hoped it would be.

Also, I found I would need some kind of shade for our hot summer sun. I didn't want my dogs bleaching out so I constructed a good wooden frame on a slant (grade) and covered it with a green colored corrugated fiberglass sheeting which runs about $7 Canadian for 26x96 inch sheets. Some people use the sheets for back porches. On a slight grade the rain and snow runs off and the green color provides cool shade. There are other colors you can use but I don't suggest light colors such as white. It will be too hot and will not provide good shade.

Up in Eastern Canada we have another serious problem as all of Eastern North America has...Heart worms. I find planting or putting citronella plant and marigolds nearby keep the mosquitoes away. Make sure the plants are out of reach from those fun loving pups and dogs!

My last helpful idea is to dust with Sevin 5% dust about twice a week to always keep ahead of ticks, lice or whatever. Just remove all animals and sweep it into cracks of the runs where little critters like to hide. Then replace the pets. I have never seen any problems with the animals and the dust.

Maurice Hogue
Purina Pet Care Center
St. Louis, Missouri

For efficiency in cleaning and maintenance, concrete and concrete block construction is preferred and generally recommended, although frame buildings can be used satisfactorily. Dogs may chew on wood, unless it is specially protected and this not only creates an unfavorable appearance, but provides hiding places for bacteria and parasites. Wood absorbs more urine and urine odors than concrete. The wood deteriorates rapidly. The higher initial cost of a concrete and concrete block building is usually offset by lower maintenance costs, ease of cleaning, savings on insurance and general appearance.

Inside pen surfaces slope toward an inside gutter at a rate of 1/2 inch per foot. Good drainage is extremely important to any kennel facility. Nothing will cause more odor or sanitation problems than uneven floors, with pockets of standing water and urine. Therefore, an evenly-sloped surface is essential. The type of concrete finish is also important. Our specifications call for a light broom finish, brushed toward the drainage trench. A too smooth surface can be slippery for the dog and the caretaker, especially when wet. Conversely, an extremely coarse surface is difficult to keep clean and will wear down the pads on a dog's feet.

Floor heating, popular in many kennels, utilizes pipes or heated cables imbedded in the floors. Floors with this type of heating dry quickly but tend to produce more odors in poorly ventilated buildings than unheated floors. Consider installing the heat pipes or cables under 1/2 of the floor on one side of the pens. This reduces costs and provides a safety feature so that dogs can move to the cooler side if overheating occurs.

Purina recommends that label instructions be followed carefully for any detergent or disinfectant used in an animal facility. Dogs should never be allowed to drink the solution. When disinfectants are used, the surfaces should be allowed to dry before the dogs are returned to them.

Outside runs that are 6 feet wide are easier to keep clean than runs 4 feet wide. Since dogs tend to race back and forth in pens, the wider pens allow dogs to avoid droppings, usually deposited in the lower end of the pen.

Concrete is generally considered to be the best surface for most kennels. Concrete, however, contains pores and unless properly sealed may harbor parasites and bacteria. Untreated cement gives off a chalky dust which can be irritating to the skin, eyes and lungs of pets. When sealing concrete make absolutely sure that the sealant is completely dry and washed prior to letting the dogs have access to it. The toxic matter in the sealant can cause serious damage when absorbed through the pads of the dog's feet.

Concrete runs should have a smooth slope of 1/2 inch to every foot of length.

Studies of dogs raised on different surfaces showed that dogs weighing over 35 pounds, who were raised on smooth concrete, developed flat and splayed feet.

Asphalt is another surface that can be used for kennel runs, but it has several disadvantages and is generally not recommended. It absorbs heat and can become extremely hot in direct sunlight on summer days.

Gravel can be used satisfactorily where ample drainage is available and gravel is 6 to 8 inches deep. It permits parasite eggs and urine to leak through and be washed away. On hot days however, dogs may dig down through the gravel to the cool layer underneath. And, when ample slope is provided for the efficient use of gravel runs, dogs have a tendency to work the gravel from the highest end to the lower end. In runs that are almost level, it is not unusual to see gravel piled a foot or more higher at each end than at the center. This is caused by dogs running and turning at each end of the run.

One method that works well and seems to have few shortcomings involves sinking concrete blocks on end as close together as possible so that the holes in the blocks drain down into the ground. The blocks are covered with several inches of pea gravel. This surface provides excellent drainage and is suitable for any climate.

Kennel Ideas

When fencing, keep the bottom support at least 1 inch above the run floor so that waste material can be flushed underneath.

<u>Pet Emergency First Aid Videos</u>

If you want to be better prepared to handle emergencies involving dogs and cats, there is a wonderful video available from the below company. Videos are priced at $19.95 and are approximately 41 minutes long.

Apogee Videos
159 Alpine Way
Boulder, Colorado 80304

Tel. No. 1-888-380-9966

Deciding On A Plan

Kennel structures can fall into any price range the kennel owners' desires, from a $250 kennel to a $100,000 kennel. No one can decide for another how much money should be spent for the welfare of his dogs.

The kennel builder who desires much more than just a typical nice kennel, may find the services of a good architect well worth the expense, especially if the kennel needs to blend with another structure both in quality as well as materials.

Should an architect be consulted, keep in mind that you know much more about dogs than he probably does. Be prepared with ideas of your own and requirements for the dogs that you want included in the kennel to submit to the architect before he begins his task of designing the "perfect" kennel for you.

Site Preparation

If you are starting from "scratch" on a new kennel you will want to determine the best possible building site on the given area you have to work with. The soil characteristics; and slope of the land will make a big difference in where the kennel will be located.

Determine where north and south are by using a compass. By sketching out your plans on a piece of graph paper you will be way ahead of the game. Indicate landmarks such as trees, large rocks, fence lines or buildings and mark your compass directions.

An easy way to measure the slope of the land is to drive a stake at the top of the slope and tie a 10 foot length of string to it at ground level. Make a loop in the other end of the string and place it around the top of another stake. Walk down the slope stretching the string tight. Level the string by holding a level on it. Measure the distance at the string height to the ground. If the string ends up being 12 inches off the ground then the slope is referred to as 1:10 (1 foot of drop in 10 feet). This measurement will help you determine the length of poles you will need and how deep to set them.

Dig several holes around the building site to determine what type characteristics the soil has. A well-drained sub-soil with a high content of sand makes an excellent base. Wet soil with a high clay content is not as desirable. It simply doesn't drain.

The direction you build your kennel is important. Since the sun, shade and direction of prevailing winds determine the comfort of your dogs, they should be first and foremost in your thoughts. Proper use of a southern exposure in northern climates means situating the kennel with the majority of the windows on the south side to take advantage of the sun's heat, reducing the winter fuel bills. A southern exposure will also provide more light in the winter. Since the sun is low in the sky in the winter, make sure that trees or other buildings don't block the sun's rays at this height.

In southern climates, the use of shade in the kennel is just as important as sun is to northern climates. Deciduous trees that leaf out in the summer, yet are bare in the winter, provide ample shade when needed yet allow the warmth to flow through them when it's cold. Don't overdo it, however. Too much shade would encourage constant dampness when the weather is moist. Trees planted on the west side of the kennel would provide relief from the afternoon sun during the summer.

A kennel that is built so that it runs lengthwise from north to south, yet has runs extending both east and west, allows the dog to absorb the morning sun and afternoon shade in the summer in the east wing and can fully absorb the sun on cold days from the west wing.

If it's only possible to provide runs in one direction, they should be on the eastern-most side for a kennel running north and south, and on the southern side for a kennel running east to west. Since Winds are normally from the North, the ideal kennel in northern climates would be situated facing south and located on the south side of any slope. Locating the kennel at the top of a hill would expose it to constantly blowing winds.

If security in your area is a problem, the kennel should be located out of site behind a larger building such as a garage or home. Not only does the building in front provide privacy, but it also helps to buffer the noise of any barking dogs.

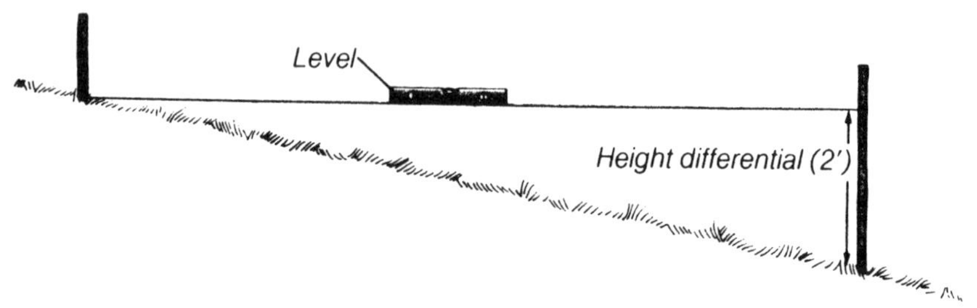

Building Materials

Lumber

Before building a kennel using lumber, stop and think about whether your particular breed is going to have a feast destroying the kennel before you've even gotten finished building it. Some dogs are such malicious chewers that they can mutilate a 2x4 piece of lumber in minutes. If this sounds like your pride and joy, then it would be better to stick to concrete block.

Don't overlook the possibility of using used lumber. If money is in short supply to cover all of the extras you really want and need, it pays to cut costs wherever you can and still have a nice kennel when you're through. Boards may get brittle and dry with age however. To test the boards to see if they are still sturdy prop one end up on something low to the ground and stand on it to see if it flexes or breaks.

Treated lumber needs to be kept away from any place the dog may have access for chewing on it. The preservatives in pressure-treated lumber are toxic to pets if ingested and could cause serious problems. Most pressure-treated wood is impregnated with a solution containing chromated copper arsenate (CCA), a compound of arsenic.

Log Home Builders have discovered that Borate based wood treatments are an excellent substitution for CCA in treating wood. Borate based wood treatments make the wood resistant to bugs & wood destroying fungi, as well as killing termites, carpenter ants, cockroaches, powder-post beetles as well as silverfish. The borate compound doesn't cost much, doesn't change the color of the wood, is easily applied and provides fire resistance.

Termites nibble at the borate treated wood and die once the cellulose-digesting protozoa and bacteria in their gut is killed. The poison is carried back to the nest and the whole colony is often wiped out.

Since borate is water-soluble some formulations can be brushed or sprayed on, instead of being applied under pressure. The only drawback to its solubility is the fact that extended contact with water can make it lose its effectiveness. The leaching can be prevented or slowed down by applying a water repellent to the surface of the borate-treated wood and re-applying every few years. The product is available directly to consumers and is found in a product called "Bora-Care" made by Perma-Chink Systems, Inc. made for log homes. It is sold as a concentrate and is diluted with equal volumes of water.

For additional information about preserving lumber you can contact:

The American Wood Preservers Assoc.
P.O. Box 849
Stevensville, Maryland 21666
Tel. No. (301) 643-4163

For more information about *"Bora-Care"* write or call:

Perma-Chink
1605 Prosser Road
Knoxville, Tennessee 37914
Tel. No. (800) 548-3554

"Tim-Bor" is another product similar to *"Bora-Care"*. It, however, needs to be applied to wood with a high moisture content. For information write or call:

U.S. Borax Company
3075 Wilshire Blvd.
Los Angeles, California 90052
Tel. No. (213) 251-5400

Lumber Dimensions

It's common now to space framing on 24" centers instead of 16" centers. The 16" spacing was a waste of money because the kind of strength it created was not necessary, especially in side walls.

Plan your building so that dimensions fit the common sizes of lumber to prevent a lot of wasted lumber. A 16' wall makes more sense than a 15' wall if you have to cut a foot off of each board and trim pieces of paneling. Try to make most dimensions divisible by 4 to get the most for your money when building.

It's usually cheaper to buy longer boards and cut them into desired lengths such as a 16' board cut in half to make two 8' boards.

Concrete

Sand, portland cement, and gravel are the dry ingredients that make up concrete. The portland cement is the binder and the sand and gravel provide the strength and space. Water is the catalyst in concrete and when added starts the chemical process (hydration) that hardens the concrete. A soupy mixture (too much water) will result in weak concrete. Also concrete loses its strength if it's allowed to dry out too quickly. In extremely dry weather keep freshly poured concrete wet by misting lightly with water or lightly covering with damp burlap or polyethylene for up to a week. Freezing weather causes air pockets unless an additive is mixed in with the concrete.

To soften the color of concrete and make it more natural looking, powdered paint pigments can be added while mixing the cement with water. It takes very little of this pigment. Add just a little and add if the color is still not intense enough. Be sure to add the pigment and blend it before the rock or gravel is added so that it won't be too difficult. To save money on pigment where you are pouring a large pad, add the pigment to only the top layer of cement you are pouring.

To remove tough pet stains from concrete driveways, apply a solution of chlorine bleach and water to the area on a sunny day. Let dry.

Working With Concrete

Concrete is measured by the cubic yard, a volume which measures 3x3x3 feet or 27 cubic feet.

By using the following formula you should be able to fairly easily determine the amount of concrete necessary for laying the kennel flooring, footings and walkways.

A slab of concrete which measures 18x18 feet and you wish to be 4 inches thick would be calculated as follows:

$$\text{Volume} = \frac{18\text{x}18\text{x}1/3 \text{ foot}}{27} = \frac{108}{27} = 4 \text{ cubic yards}$$

A slab of concrete which measures 20x30 feet and you wish to be 6 inches thick would be calculated:

$$\text{Volume} = \frac{20\text{x}30\text{x}1/2 \text{ foot}}{27} = \frac{300}{27} = 11.1 \text{ cubic yards}$$

Unbelievable as it seems, a cubic yard of concrete would require about fifty 80 lb. bags of pre-mixed concrete.

Mixing your own concreteis easy and inexpensive. A cubic yard of concrete mixed from scratch costs about $35. To do it yourself, call your local sand quarry and tell them you need sand and gravel mix for mixing your own concrete. Combine this with Portland cement you can buy from a lumberyard or home building supply store. Thoroughly mix 1 shovelful of cement to 5 shovelfuls of sand and gravel. Once mixed to a uniform color, add water to create the right consistancy.

It would be fairly safe to assume that any job requiring over 1 cubic yard should be referred to your local concrete dealer and delivered by truck already mixed for you.

Delivered concrete runs about $48 to $60 per yard.

How Much Concrete Do You Need to Fill a Post Hole?

The depth of concrete should equal at least half the depth of the hole. It's a waste of money to fill the hole all the way to the top of the soil.

Small jobs

(couple of posts)
Use pre-mixed concrete in 1 cubic foot bags
Add water, mix in wheelbarrow

Medium Sized jobs (up to 1 cu. yard or 27 cu. feet)
Purchase portland cement in 1 cu. foot bags
Purchase sand & gravel
Mix in portable mixer (rent one) or mix by hand

Large jobs (greater than 1 cu. yard)
Have ready-made concrete delivered
(Usually runs around $48 to $60 per yard)

*Be sure to allow about 10% for waste.

<u>As another example:</u> 1 cubic yard will pour a 10 x10' slab that is 3 inches thick.

Concrete Block & Bricks

Concrete block structures are long-lasting, easy to maintain and are quick to build with the help of a good block mason. The concrete block building will still be around long after the wood framed kennel has been taken over by termites or simply rotted away.

If you can't stand the appearance of a block building, cover it with brick or siding to match a surrounding building such as your home. The strength and durability will make it a worthwhile choice.

Standard bricks are 4" wide by 8" long and 2 1/2" thick. The darker the red in the brick, the more durable.

How much mortar Will You Need?

1 cubic foot of mortar will lay about 30 cinder blocks (8"x8"x16") or 70 bricks (2"x4"x8").

Be sure to mix only enough for approximately 1 hours worth of work. (It drys out)

Mortar contains cement, lime and sand to bond masonry. It contains no gravel. The hydrated lime slows down the set up by retaining water in the mixture.

Rolled Heavy Gauge Aluminum Sheeting

To protect any wooden surface that the dog is prone to chew on in the kennel area, rolled heavy gauge aluminum sheeting can be used to line the lower portion of walls. Rolls of sheeting are available at most home building warehouse stores, recreational vehicle or mobile home supply stores, farm supply stores and often from your local heating & air conditioning dealers.

The sheeting is waterproof, chew proof, easily hosed down, easy to disinfect and can be readily fastened to a wall. Retail price on a 50 foot roll of 19 gauge aluminum sheeting 36" wide runs about $50 -- $65.

Patio Blocks

Garden shops and hardware stores carry 12"x12" or larger patio blocks in a variety of shapes, sizes and colors. For temporary kennels, or as a good substitute for poured concrete in outdoor runs, patio blocks are quick to install and easy to remove for a change in design or move to another location. Adding to the kennel is also a breeze. The blocks tend to dry faster than cement after getting wet because of their porosity. Don't forget to look in the local yellow pages for a nearby cement manufacturer who may sell them to you direct at wholesale. "Seconds" often sell for only 50 cents each if you do your own picking-up and hauling from their reject piles.

Wooden Patio Squares

Now that decks are so popular, building supply stores often carry 4'x4' wooden patio squares for do-it-yourselfers who are putting together outdoor patio decks. They run about $10 each for this size and would be worth considering for use as resting benches for the dogs instead of purchasing the lumber and building them yourself. The only drawback is that they are most often manufactured out of treated lumber...good for longevity, but questionable as to the long-term health of the dog after constant exposure to the preservative in the wood. If treated with Pentachlorophenol (Penta for short) it is extremely toxic to animals as well as plants and humans.

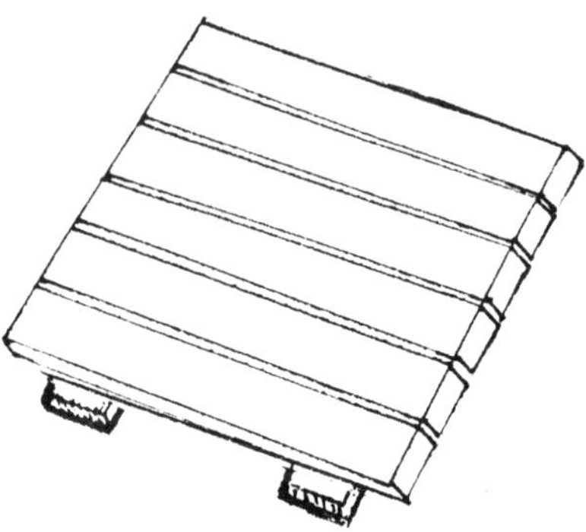

Kennel Stall Doors

By installing kennel stall doors so that they open inwardly, you help thwart the dog who likes to escape at any opportunity. By also raising the door at least a foot above the floor level, with a solid panel beneath it, you can avoid injuring any small pups. The door will swing open above them and prevent head bashing.

If ample room permits, aluminum storm doors make excellent stall doors. Most come with a top panel that can be lowered to expose screening for more ventilation on hot summer days. The aluminum lasts longer and the glass top permits easy viewing of the stall within. Larger breeds of dogs would prohibit the use of the glass panel on top however, because of possible glass shattering when they jump up.

Interior & Exterior Doors

Interior doors are put together with interior glue whereas exterior doors are put together with exterior glue so that they can withstand the weather. Exterior doors are 1 3/4" thick to keep them from warping compared to only 1 3/8" for interior doors. Remember to always finish both sides of a door. Putting a sealer on only one side will often cause the door to warp because of moisture buildup.

Kennel Nesting Box Doors

Simple doors can be constructed for the dog to go in and out of his dog house. With a simple top hinged door it is possible to manipulate the door without entering the kennel at all by the caretaker. The pulley is placed at least twice the height of the door from the floor.

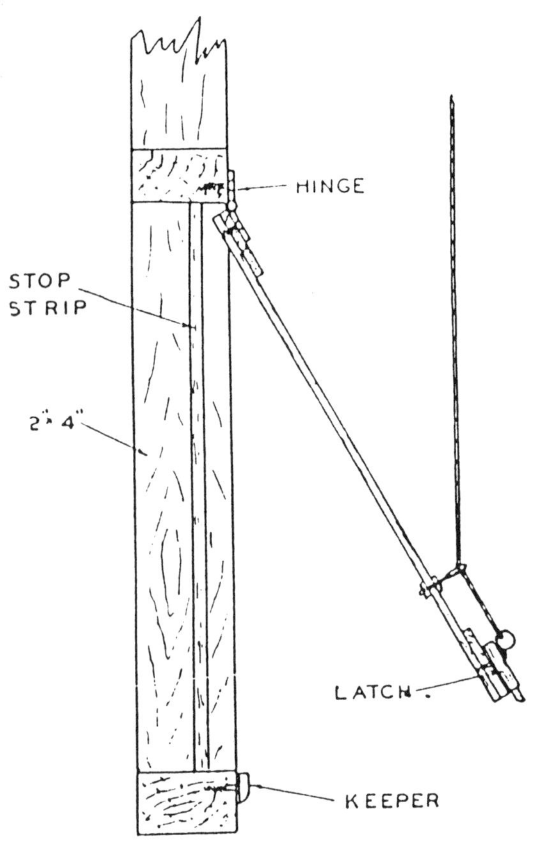

This door can be opened & closed from outside of the stall. The line that operates the latch is passed overhead through pulleys in some convenient place so that it can be reached.

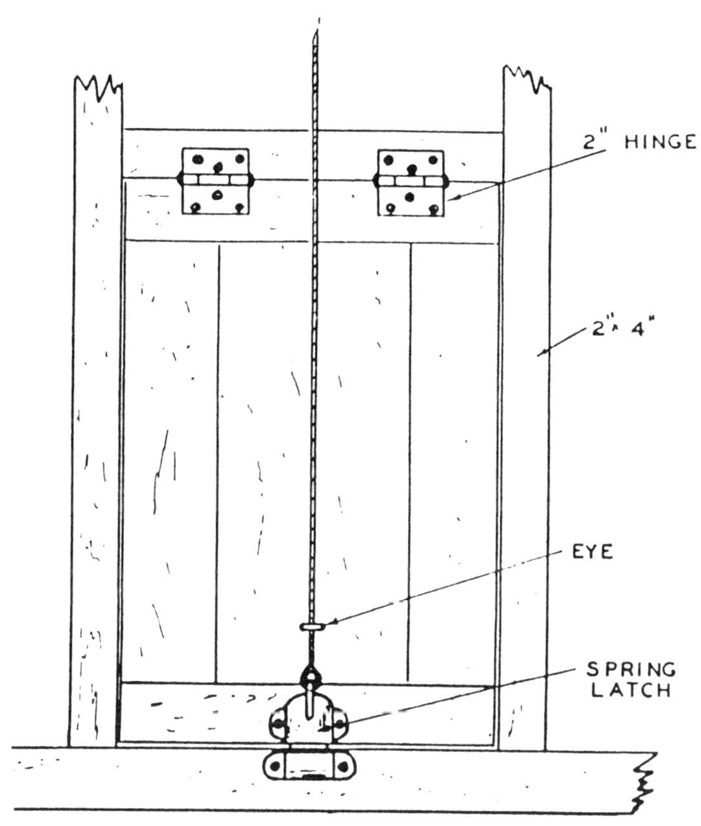

Getting The Most For Your Money

Discounts are available on almost all products. To get the discount a simple "What kind of discount do you offer?" is all that is necessary. When an item gets above $30 it's often time to start negotiating.

Buying in bulk usually saves you money unless you cannot ever use what's left over. Then you've actually not saved anything. Loose items are generally less expensive than packaged groups of items or carded items such as screws and washers. There are exceptions to this rule such as hinges. A box of hinges is around 5 percent cheaper than loose ones.

Nails are always cheaper when bought in bulk beginning with the 1 pound box and getting less expensive when you purchase 50 pound boxes. Rope is cheaper in short lengths if purchased by the foot off a large roll. For longer lengths (over 25 feet) look for packaged rope and save money. Store any leftover lengths by hanging it up to keep it from rotting.

Aluminum screening comes in different gauges based on strength. The heavier gauge, 18x14 is excellent for those instances where you expect some wear & tear. Use the lighter gauge, 18x16, in protected areas. Buying screening by the package instead off a roll in bulk is quite a bit more expensive.

Fiberglass screening won't deteriorate when exposed to water. It looks great but it can tear and is generally not as strong.

Hardware cloth (mesh wire) comes in widths between two feet and 4 feet and is generally sold by the foot off of large rolls. Try to buy galvanized wire that is galvanized after the material is woven. Pre-galvanized wire is inferior because the strands of wire are spot welded and are not as weather resistant.

Chains

Chain comes in various strengths referred to as SWL (safe working load). Be sure to match the chain strength to the job. Galvanized chain will last for many years whereas plain, non-galvanized will readily rust in a short period of time.

Nuts, bolts, screws

Galvanized nuts, bolts and screws will be more expensive but won't rust as fast. Galvanizing makes them impervious to the weather. In a kennel this will be important because of the constant exposure to moisture. A true galvanized item has a rough, dull gray finish as compared to a shiny finish of an item that is electro-plated or non-galvanized.

Tear off a strip of masking tape and lay flat, sticky side up when taking an item apart that has several small parts. Line the parts up on the masking tape in the order that they are removed so that re-assembly is easier.

Paintbrushes & roller trays

Cheap paintbrushes and rollers don't really save money in the long run. The time spent pulling loose bristles and fiber out of wet paint is frustrating. Foam brushes are excellent for interior trim work but don't work well on exterior oil-based paints.

An easy way to store a wet oil-based paint brush is to stick it in a can of water overnight. In the morning when you are ready to paint, simply blot off water and resume the job. The water prevents any oxygen from getting to the paint and doesn't let it dry. Alkyd primers are the best when trying to get paint to solidly adhere to a surface, even though you may be using a latex top coat. Latex paint <u>will</u> adhere to an alkyd primer. Do you know what the difference is between alkyd paint and oil based paint? The alkyd paint is relatively odor-free and adheres to all other paints on wood. It drys slower than latex however and is not really good for masonry or wallboard.

When painting overhead, slip the handle of the brush through a hole pierced in the center of a paper plate and secure it with a piece of tape. Any drips will land on the paper plate instead of down your arm or face.

Stretch a large rubber band from top to bottom around the middle of an open paint to give you something to scrape excess paint from your brush each time you dip.

Use an old shower curtain or liner as a drop cloth instead of the flimsy plastic sheeting that is sold for that purpose. The shower curtain is more durable and lays much flatter. Shower curtain liners are usually only $3 - $4 dollars.

To protect your watch while painting cover the face with a piece of clear cellophane tape till done. You can still read the time, but the face is protected.

The one-coat rollers save both time and money. Though they cost more they save you more in the long run since in most cases you can get by with one coat of paint saving both paint and labor.

The new plastic roller trays are wonderful! Wet or dried paint can easily be removed with either warm water soapy water for latex paints or mineral spirits for oil-based paints. They seem to last for years and are actually cheaper.

Tape Measures and Rules

Buy at least a 25 foot tape measure with a 1 inch width instead of a 3/4 inch width. The smaller width is much too flimsy for most jobs.

Gutters

Buy 5" wide gutters instead of 4" whenever available. The wider gutter makes up for being more expensive by being able to handle greater quantities of water.

Vinyl guttering is cheaper than aluminum seamless guttering but tends to expand and contract causing more leaks.

Homemade Dog Biscuits

1/2 cup cornmeal
6 Tbsp cooking oil
2 cups whole wheat flour
2/3 cup chicken or beef broth

Preheat oven to 350 degrees. Mix all ingredients well. Roll out to 1/4 inch thick. Cut into desired shapes with cookie cutter. Bake 35-40 minutes. Let cool, then store in airtight container.

Nails & Nailing

It's better to nail a thinner board to a thick board for strength. The depth of penetration should be at least twice the thickness of the thinner board.

To avoid splitting the wood near the edge or end of a board, blunt the pointed end of nail with a couple of taps of a hammer before driving it in. This forces a hole as it's driven instead of forcing the fibers apart and splitting.

Bathtubs

Fiberglass bathtubs which have been slightly damaged in shipping or warehousing, are often available at local plumbing supply stores for a fraction of the cost of new ones. In fact, some stores give them away. It doesn't hurt to inquire.

A hair dryer can be used as a makeshift blower to clean small areas such as window sills or floorboards, by flipping to the air only setting.

Roofing

Most roofing materials are measured by the square which is an area 10 x 10 feet or 100 square feet.

Asphalt or asbestos shingles are sold in bundles. It takes 3 bundles to equal a square. The heavier the shingle the better the quality.

To find out how many shingles you need simply measure the square footage of both sides of the roof (multiply length times width) and divide by 100. This tells you the total number of squares you will need. Add some to this figure for waste and ridge caps.

Tar paper to go under the shingles comes in 3-foot wide rolls that are 144 feet long. Each roll covers 4 squares. You'll also need galvanized roofing nails at the rate of 2-3 pounds per square of roof area.

Metal roofing, either galvanized or aluminum comes in common widths of 32 inches to cover 30 inches of roof and 38 inches to cover 36 inches of roof once properly overlapped. To figure the amount needed multiply the net width by the length of the sheets.

Heating The Kennel

Most dogs like it cool. Just watch them when a break in the weather produces a little chill in the air after the hot days of summer. They run, jump and get a renewed vitality from the change in temperature. Compare this to the hot summer days when they lie around sleeping and act as if they have absolutely no energy to get up, much less eat and play.

Too much heat can cause laziness, lack of appetite, obesity, poor coats, tendency to colds and viruses and skin problems.

Dogs taken from too warm a kennel to the outdoors during the winter and subjected to cold temperatures are subject to the same stress as humans, only they have no jackets and hats on to keep them insulated from the extreme differences n temperatures.

Not only is heating equipment expensive to purchase, but it is also expensive to operate and maintain. Any heating equipment installed should be thermostatically controlled and kept between 50 and 72 degrees.

An alternative to heating the air in the kennel would be to insulate the building well to prevent drafts and dampness and use radiant heat in the wall, floors and ceilings. A heat mat for each dog would also be less expensive in the long run, since heat would be available at the cost of a light bulb, when needed by the resting dog.

A room set aside for grooming should definitely be heated to provide a warm place for bathing the dogs when necessary in the winter. By making the grooming room only as big as absolutely necessary, very little electricity is required to heat it.

Whatever source of heat you use, keep it well-maintained and safe. A malfunctioning heater can burn an entire kennel up in minutes. Keep fire extinguishers handy, and provide an emergency exit in addition to the main entrance to the kennel.

Rely on the sun for the cheapest source of heat. Windows located on the south and east sides of the kennel can provide an abundance of natural heat in the winter.

Keep the kennel ventilated. An "airing out," on the nicest of wintry days, can do wonders for accumulated odors in the kennel.

> Spray the bottom of your dogs paws with a non-stick cooking spray to keep snow and ice from packing between his toes on icy days.

Fencing

The height of the fence necessary to properly kennel dogs varies with the breed. Toy dogs would do well with 2 foot fencing whereas larger breeds need at least 6 foot fencing to keep them from jumping out.

Chainlink

Chainlink fencing is available in a variety of sizes and gauges so shop around. The lower the gauge of fencing, the strongcr thc wirc. One inch mesh, 16 gauge chainlink fencing is preferred by most breeders of small to medium sized dogs, whereas 14 gauge wire would be more practical for large, strong willed dogs. By choosing 1 inch mesh instead of the less expensive 2 inch, you prevent the dogs from fighting through the wire with others and prevent a lot of accidents involving stuck paws, broken teeth, bitten noses, etc.

An alternative to costly new chainlink fencing is to check with local fence building companies to see if they sell used chainlink fencing which has been removed from other jobs they've replaced. Used chainlink fencing is often available for less than half of the cost of new and can be restored to a new looking finish with the application of a coat of galvanized paint. It's easy to repaint using either a spray can, a roller, or as one fence dealer suggested..the use of an old absorbant glove to apply the paint by hand, making it easy to thoroughly saturate all of the little crevices in the fencing.

Woven Wire

Fencing around the perimeter of the kennel can be of strong woven wire fencing. Woven wire comes in different gauges just like chainlink fencing.

The bottom of the fence should extend into the ground for 6 to 10 inches to prevent the dogs from digging out. Woven wire is available in either rolls or panels of different lengths and heights, depending upon your needs. By using a 2x4 inch triangular or diamond mesh type fence, with cross wires, you can prevent the dogs from climbing the fence.

In areas of high visibility, some type of wood board fencing or solid panel fencing might be preferred. Solid fencing also provides a wind break for the dogs. By cutting down on the visibility of the dogs, barking is also reduced.

WIRE FENCING TYPES

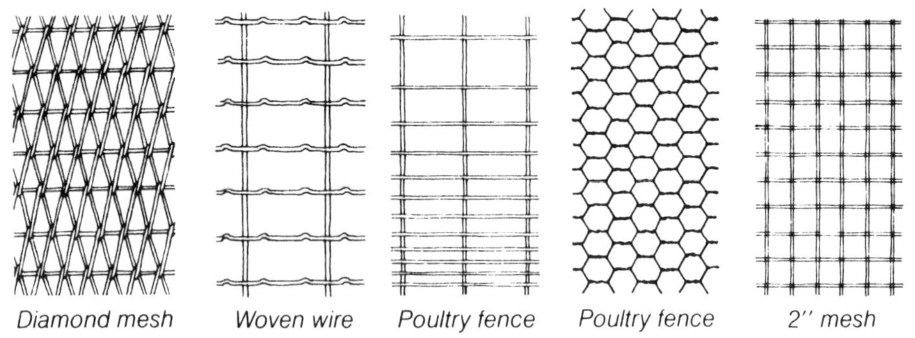

Diamond mesh *Woven wire* *Poultry fence* *Poultry fence* *2'' mesh*

Board Fencing

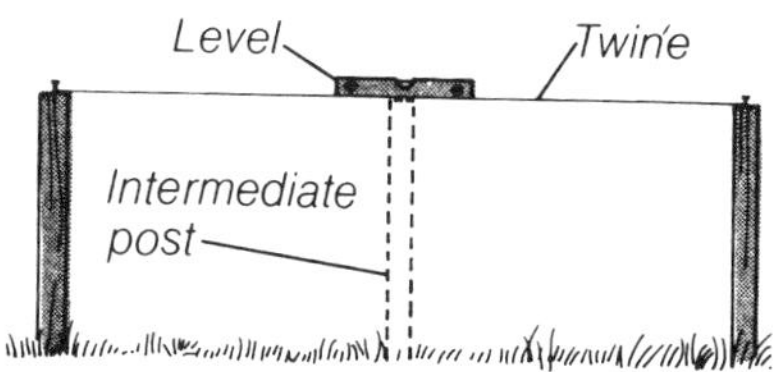

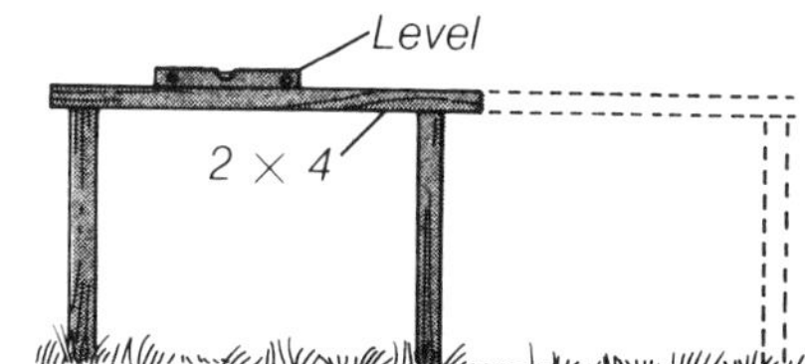

SETTING POSTS

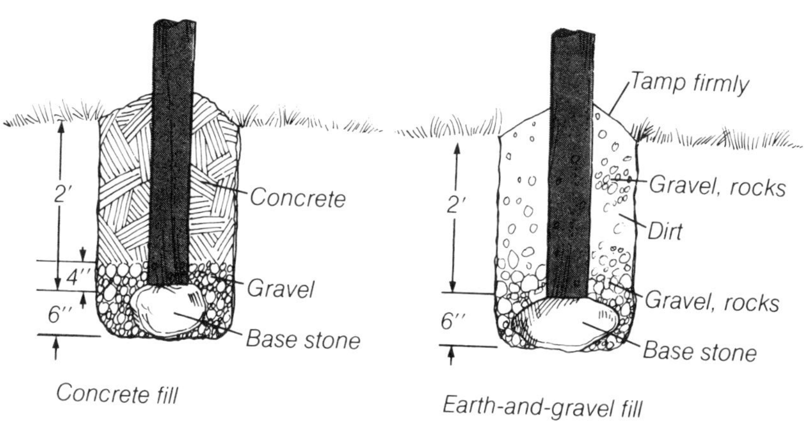

Concrete fill

Earth-and-gravel fill

TYPICAL BOARD FENCE

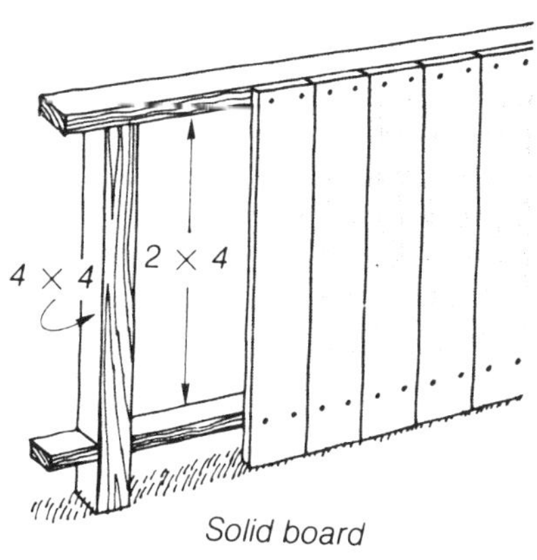

Solid board

Electronic Fencing

If you need to be a little creative with your fencing requirements, electronic fencing may be the answer. Perhaps you live in a condominium and can't put up a fence because of association by-laws, or for one reason or another, you need a way to prohibit your dog(s) from having access to an area of the yard where flowers are planted or small children are playing...electronic fencing may be the solution.

Electronic fencing is an underground electrical barrier that works with a receiver on your dog's collar. It beeps your dog when he nears the boundary and gives him a small electrical correction if he tries to cross it. It keeps your dog safe and out of trouble without having to resort to expensive fences, ropes, cages or chains.

The fencing works with any size or breed of dog. The correction that is similar to a static electricity charge, will not hurt your pet.

In just hours you can install enough wire to accommodate a half-acre yard. The transmitter signal is powerful enough to have a range of approximately 1,000 square feet. You can train your dog(s) in usually a week's time. Once your pet has learned the boundaries, the electric charge may be removed off of his collar, allowing only the chirping sound to alert him when he is too near the boundary.

The transmitter plugs into an ordinary outlet in your home and emits a radio signal that travels along an underground wire that is buried only an inch or two beneath the ground.

Price starts around $150 for a complete system.

An excellent place to start looking for it would be building supply houses such as Home Depot, Lowes or stores such as Petsmart.

Pros: Inexpensive
Can be installed around plants and trees
suitable when fencing is not allowed due to homeowner restrictions

Cons: Neighbors dogs can still visit
"Gutsy" dog may go through anyway
Won't protect dog "in-heat"

Dog Houses

Place the dog house in a sheltered area out of the weather. Near a building, or up against one provides the best protection.

When building, use a design that provides for easy cleaning, such as a roof that hinges upward for both ventilation on hot days and airing out and cleaning. Be sure to have some sort of fastening down hook so that strong winds don't blow it open.

Locate the door of the dog house to one side so that the dog is isolated from strong winds and rain on the sheltered side.

When determining size, smaller is best. Too large a house in the winter will be cold. The dog gives off enough body heat to adequately heat himself unless the house is too large. Keep it just large enough for the dog to curl up in it when cold. For small dogs an area of 18"x24" is usually sufficient; for medium dogs, 24"x24"; and for larger dogs 36"x48." Stretching out room is usually not necessary since the dog, on nice days, will be snoozing elsewhere.

A separate compartment in the dog house assures warmth and security. The dog enters a vestibule area then goes around a wall for the next box area. With a slanted roof, the nest box area can be located in the low end of the house. When lying down, not much head room is necessary.

Color can be important. White dog houses stay around 15 to 20 degrees cooler than dark colored ones in hot weather. Dark dog houses stay 6 to 10 degrees warmer in the winter.

A flat roof, or just slightly sloped roof, provides the dog a resting bench on nice days.

A 6 inch board at the base of the doorway helps keep shavings or other bedding inside the dog house.

Make sure the dog house does not sit directly on the cement or ground. By raising it off the surface by at least a few inches, you create a dead air space for extra warmth. This area needs to be boxed in to protect it from drafts and to keep small pups from getting trapped underneath.

Check the bedding frequently to make sure it is clean and dry.

Keep in mind that dog house roofs fabricated out of tin or metal may build up too much heat within. Stick your head inside or place a thermometer inside on a hot day to find out whether you need to re-roof with another type material such as fiberglass shingles.

Whelping Pens

Location

Try to locate the whelping pen in separate quarters. By locating the whelping pen away from the rest of the kennel, not only will peace and quiet be maintained for the new family, but the new pups will have a better start in life if kept away from any prevailing illness in the rest of the kennel.

The location chosen should be draft-free, neither too hot, nor too cold and above all, not damp. By locating the whelping pen area convenient to the caretaker, the pups stand a better chance of being checked on more easily and more often. With an area set aside in the house or basement, you have the added advantage of not having to "brave" the weather on cold, wet days & nights.

Temperature

Temperature for the whelping area should be at least 70 - 80 degrees. This is especially true for the first 10 days when the whelps do not have the ability to warm themselves through shivering.

The best indication of how warm or cold the pups are is whether they are sprawled out comfortably sleeping, or whether they are huddled in a pile trying to get warm. Pups should feel pleasantly warm to the touch when felt.

After about two weeks, pups should be able to withstand temperatures around 60 degrees, as long as there is not any dampness or drafts. Overheated kennels can probably cause more ills than underheated, draft-free, dry ones.

Warming Mats

A Warming mat will provide gentle heat for the pups yet allow the room to be at a lower temperature for the dam's comfort. Simply turning up the temperature in the room to accommodate the new pups makes it difficult on the new mom to acclimate to the warmer temperatures and perform her duties well without undue stress.

When using warming mats, be sure the pups do not become dehydrated from too much heat. A thermometer can be used to check on the temperature of the mat to insure that the pups are not being kept too hot. Sometimes simply hanging the mat over the edge of the whelping box, so that the pups can back up to its warmth, is adequate.

Several warming mats are on the market by different manufacturers. The least expensive are those manufactured for baby piglets. Most mats on the market have available for an additional cost a separate thermostat control which allows you to manually adjust the mat to the desired temperature.

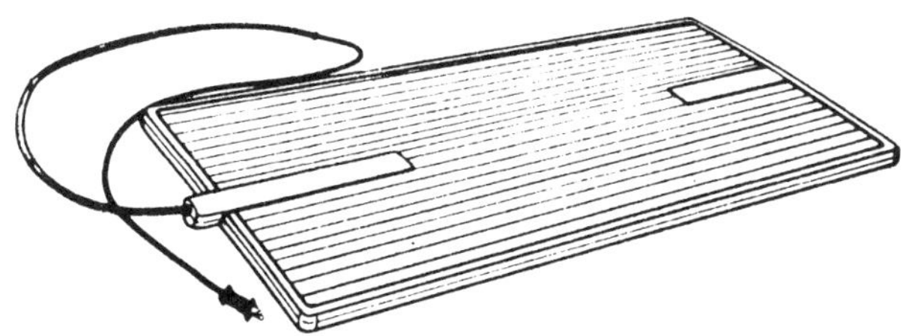

Kennel Ideas

A 12" x 18" mat is more than large enough to provide heat for the average sized litter. By having the mat smaller than the box they are in, they are able to move on and off the mat as they need to for warmth. A mat which is too large, which covers the entire floor area of their pen, may overheat and cause the death of the pups if the thermostat malfunctions.

An especially well-made mat is made of heavy black rubber with the heating coils within. Complete immersion for cleaning is possible with this type. The cord is covered with wire coiling to prevent a shock if chewed.

Example of approximate prices in 1999:

<u>R.C. Steel Wholesale Dog Equipment & Supplies:</u>

1-800-872-3773

Lectro-Kennel Mat 16" x 22"	$58.94
Optional Thermostat	$19.98

<u>Master Animal Care</u>

1-800-346-0749 for U.S.
1-717-384-5555 outside U.S.

Lectro-Kennel Mat 12" x 18"	$49.19
Optional Thermostat	$17.49

<u>Omaha Vaccine</u>

1-800-367-4444

Lectro-Kennel Mat 12" x 18"	$41.75
Optional Thermostat	$18.35
T.E. Scott Warming Nest	$242.85

Heat Lamps

Heat lamps with infra-red bulbs can successfully be used for supplemental heat for the dam and pups if extreme precaution is used to avoid electrical hazards and overheating due to installing the bulb too close. Always check the temperature at the level of the dam and pups to make sure that it is not above approximately 75 degrees. A cord left hanging within range of chewing pups or a "stressed out" dam could be disastrous!

Privacy

Dams should be kenneled in such a way that they can get away from the demands of hungry pups when she needs a "break".

Provide the dam with a low partition that she can jump over to get away without the pups following.

Pen Size

The pen size necessary will depend upon the breed being whelped. A pen 5'x5' with sides 18" high are adequate for large breeds, whereas small breeds would be quite comfortable with a 2'x2' pen with sides only 8 - 10" high. If in doubt, always make the pen a little too large rather than too small. The dam must be able to stretch out on her side comfortably when nursing the pups.

> Use a 2 liter soda bottle as a substitute hot water bottle for a new litter of pups. Replenish as needed with warm water.

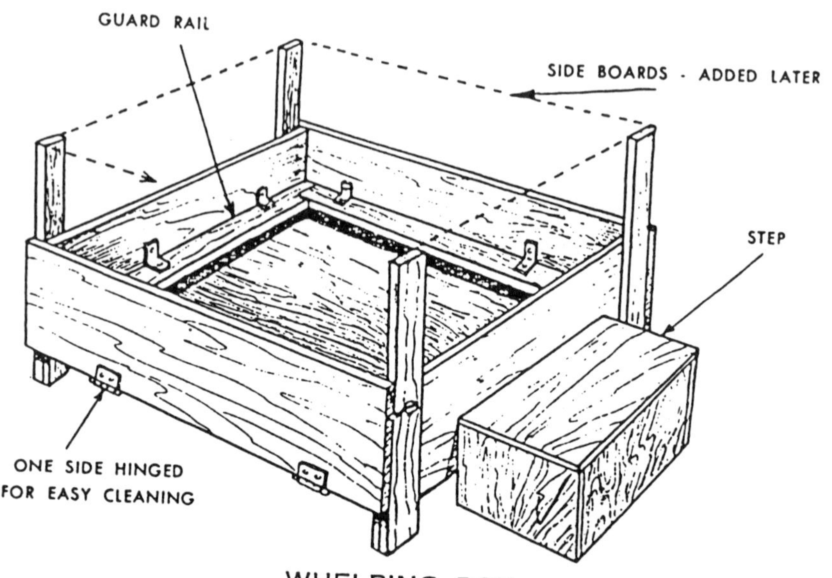

WHELPING BOX

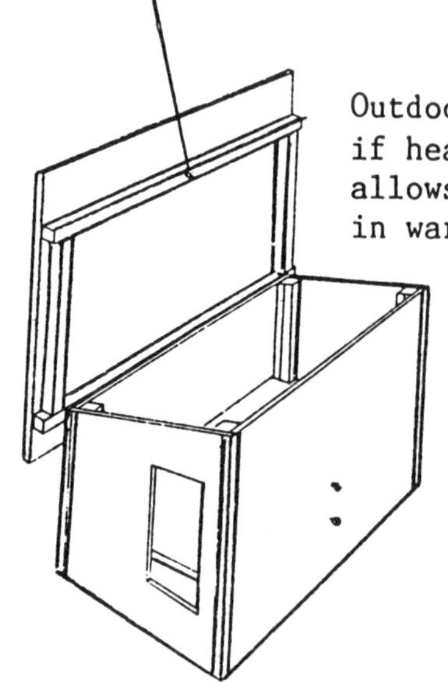

Outdoor dog box suitable for whelping if heat mat is used within. Hinged top allows for easy access and ventilation in warm weather.

Design

The design of the whelping pen can be simple or elaborate depending upon the preference of the breeder.

A welcome addition to any whelping pen is the protection given from bumper strips around the edges of the pen to keep the dam from accidentally smothering a pup by lying on it.

The bumper strip provides the pups with an escape area when the dam pushes back against the sides of the pen when she's getting "settled in". An easy way to add the bumper strips is to drill 1" holes into the sides of the corners of the whelping pen and insert 1" dowel rods through them. Holes should be drilled approximately 4 - 6" from the corners and 3 - 4" above the floor of the pen.

Bedding

Heavy towels or other fabric could accidentally trap a pup underneath. By properly fastening down the bedding however the cloth provides a warm cozy surface.

Shredded newspapers are the favorite choice of breeders. They are clean, easy to remove when soiled, cannot trap small pups, and are readily available. Newspapers have the added ability to encourage later housebreaking on newspapers since they become accustomed to their use in the whelping area.

Cedar shavings are sometimes preferred for bedding because of the nice smell they give to the pups and because some feel they repel fleas. If used, it is better to wait until the pups are several weeks old. If used too early, tiny newborns tend to get them in their mouths when nursing and swallow them. This can lead to poisoning the pups. Fine shavings can also cause eye problems in the newborns as well. A bacteria called "Klebsiella" can come from wood chips and is a serious problem when encountered. The Klebsiella bacteria gets into the wood when the logs are dragged from the forest. The bacteria remains in the wood in a dormant stage. Breeding bitches and infant pups seem to be far more susceptible to infection than other dogs.

Symptoms of infected dogs may include poor appetite, lethargy, depression, bloating, mouth ulcers, fever and often early death. Treated chips are marketed for bedding, but are sometimes difficult to find.

Whatever bedding is used, it should be changed often for dryness, cleanliness and odor control. Pups which are allowed to remain in soiled bedding for long periods of time have a difficult time later on establishing their inborn instinct of eliminating away from their "nest". A pup that smells urine all the time doesn't know what a clean bed should smell like.

During the first 10 days or so, the dam will keep the pups clean and stimulate their bowels, consuming all of the waste instinctively. After this point in time, housecleaning becomes more demanding. Puppies tend to eliminate upon each wakening and after each feeding. If unshredded newspapers are used for bedding, fresh ones can simply be added during the day on top of the soiled ones. Complete disposal of all papers should be made at least once a day however, to prevent dampness and odor build-up.

Product Sources

Kennel Pads - washable sheepskin

Cindi Reynolds
Sleepee-Time Beds
2730 Willow Oak Circle
Charlottesville, VA 22901

Tel. (804) 296-1683
Fax (804) 296-1686

Internet: www.sleepeetime.com

Dog Beds

Ortho-Bean Pet Beds 1-800-903-2326
P.O. Box 4863
Calabash, NC 28467

These beds are durable, can be used indoors or out, are easy to clean, hypo-allergenic, improve body circulation, do not promote bacterial growth, fleas and ticks cannot survive in it.

Waste Disposal

Keeping the kennel clean is first and foremost on the minds of most kennel owners. Taking pride in the way your kennel looks is well worth the effort, providing the background for healthy dogs and a proper place in which you can show off these animals to which you've devoted much time & energy.

Natural Composting

The easiest and cheapest method of disposing of dog waste is by natural decomposition. Since dog foods are made mostly of grains and meat by-products, they are biodegradable.

By disposing of dog wastes back into the soil, a natural decomposition takes place. Finicky people may disagree with this concept. The only reason, scientifically speaking, that the practice has any drawbacks, is the fact that the wastes may possibly contain germs and worms from the dog.

If good worm control is maintained on a routine basis, the risk of parasitic infestation of the soil is minimized. By having the dogs routinely checked for worms by your veterinarian and administering worm medicines when necessary, the waste material should pose no problem to the soil.

If the thought of adding the composted dog waste to the vegetable garden is repulsive, a flower garden is the perfect solution. Dig a trench where flowers are desired, putting the soil aside that came out of the hole. Wastes can be dumped daily into the trench. Cover this up immediately each day with some of the soil that is set aside. There is no odor or fly problem because you have covered the waste up immediately. For good measure throw in a handful of wood ashes or sawdust, when available, to help neutralize odors. An added benefit is that you can say good-bye to the problem of the dog who likes to dig holes in flower beds. Generally speaking, a dog won't dig where he can smell the odor of dog feces. Once the hole or trench is filled up, simply sprinkle on some flower seeds or plant shrubbery in the hole and start a new area.

Septic Systems

A septic system is a great way to dispose of the waste produced in the kennel. A septic tank is a watertight box that keeps raw sewage from entering the surrounding soil. Heavy sediment settles to the bottom of the tank and stays there, while the suspended matter floats on top where bacteria decompose it into liquid. As new liquid flows into the tank, liquid flows out of the other end of the tank through a pipe to stone-lined trenches that disperse the liquid into the soil.

If you live in a rural area where you already have a septic tank, you can easily tap into the pipe leading to the existing tank.

Larger dogs may require their own septic tank because of the volume of stool that they produce.

Generally speaking, the septic tank should be sized larger than the calculations used for humans since a dog's digestive system is not as efficient and produces more waste.

One way to hook into the existing septic system is to cement either a 6 or 8 inch diameter plastic (PVC) or terra cotta pipe (red clay) directly to the top of the septic tank, letting it extend above the soil line by a foot or so. Waste is dumped directly into the pipe and falls into the septic tank for decomposition. By using some sort of funnel on the top of the pipe, dumping the waste is less frustrating. A bucket turned upside down, or some other type of cover must be kept on the pipe at all other times in order to keep down odor and as a safety precaution. Rain water would also tend to fill up the septic system too rapidly if left uncovered.

An alternative to the pipe cemented directly to the top of the septic tank, involves a little more effort. By cutting into the main line which feeds the septic system, close to the entrance to the septic tank, a "T" fitting can be inserted and a trap assembled which does away with any odor created from the septic system. The waste is still dumped into the pipe, which extends above the soil level, yet it functions more like a traditional plumbing arrangement. Since waste must flow through the trap, it should be mixed with water first in the scoop bucket and allowed to dissolve partially to hasten the flow through the trap. A bucket of clean water can then be dumped to thoroughly push the waste material into the septic tank.

A more sophisticated waste disposal system can be set up by placing cement gutters at the end of the runs. As the runs are hosed off each day the waste material runs into the gutters and is channeled into the septic tank. Some sort of rain by-pass would have to be designed to keep too much water from entering the septic tank and destroying the enzyme action of the tank.

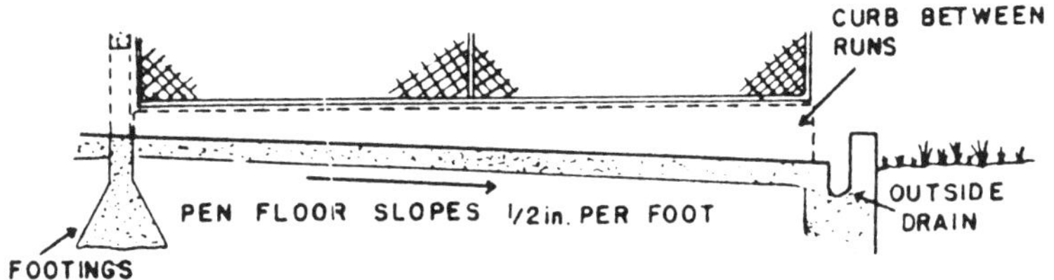

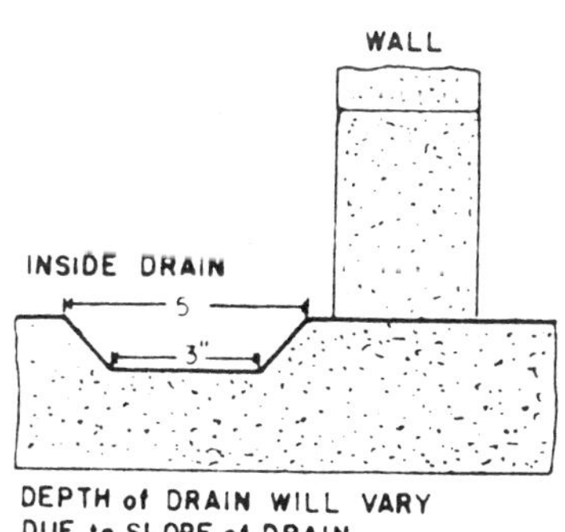

Commercial High Pressure Toilets

A commercial high pressure toilet, such as those encountered in shopping centers and other public restrooms, would work well as a disposal system for small dogs. The volume of waste produced by larger breeds would overwhelm the system. This method of disposal could be used by city dwellers who have no access to their own septic tank. Check with your plumber or local plumbing supply store for price and requirements.

Plastic Bags

For those who kennel toy or other small dogs, the disposal of wastes in plastic bags for the garbage is an accepted method. Long handled scoopers make the task easier and those which also have a plastic bag attached on the end are even better. Just be sure that the bags are securely fastened once filled and ready for disposal.

> Make a “pooper scooper”by cutting an empty bleach container in half. Use the half with the handle as the scooper and the other half to hold the droppings.

Disinfecting & Cleaning

One of the most important aspects of the kennel is its cleanliness. Disinfectants cannot work properly if the area to be disinfected is full of dirt and grime. A thorough cleaning is in order before disinfectants should be used.

Types of Disinfectants

Disinfectants fall into different categories based upon their properties. In order to properly distinguish one from another it helps to know what each provides. The following definitions are helpful:

Antiseptic - Inhibits the reproduction of micro-organisms

Deodorant - An odor improving scent added to products to improve the smell. Does not disinfect.

Bactericidal - Kills bacteria. Different disinfectants are effective agains certain bacteria such as Staph, Strep, Salmonella, pseudomonas, E. Coli and others. Check the label for what the disinfectant kills.

Bacteriostatic - May stop the growth of certain bacteria, but does not kill them.

Viricidal - Kills viruses. Read the label to see which viruses the particular disinfectant kills.

Disinfectant - Inactivates or destroys microorganisms. Read the label to see which microorganisms are covered.

Detergent - Cleanser. Does not kill microorganisms.

Fungicidal - Kills fungi. Read label to see which ones are covered.

Germicidal - Not specific enough to be effectively relied upon.

Sanitizer - A chemical that reduces the number of microorganisms to a level that is less likely to cause health problems.

Sterilization - A process that kills all forms of microorganisms. There is no liquid disinfectant in the world that can every truly sterilize.

Chlorine Bleach

Chlorine bleach, when properly diluted in a 1:30 part solution, is a good disinfectant for viruses, funguses and bacteria. Effective in both hard and soft water, it remains active when mixed with soaps. Chlorine bleach however has no residual activity.

Iodine

Iodine mixed with alcohol is effective against viruses, funguses and bacteria. It is not effective in hard water though it does have some residual activity.

Infections From Pets

Your pet could be the culprit if you or your family members keep coming down with recurrent streptococcal sore throats. To be safe, have your vet do a throat culture on any suspected dogs to verify that you are not getting re-infected by a dog in the kennel.

Getting Insects Out of Ears

According to the American Medical Association, the best way to get a live, buzzing insect out of your ear is to float it out. Turn the occupied ear up and pour water or mineral oil into the ear canal.

Other Solutions That Work

Stool Eating -"Coprohagia"

By sprinkling monosodium glutamate moderately on the food of all of the dogs in the kennel, stool eating is generally stopped. A handy source for monosodium glutamate is meat tenderizer, such as "Accent", which can be found at your local grocery store in the spice section. The resulting flavor of the stool is altered in such a way that the dogs refuse to eat them any longer.

Another product to look for is called "Forbid".

Hook Worms

The product Borax, found in the laundry section of the grocery store, spread on the soil at the rate of 1 pound per 10 square feet, will kill hookworm eggs. It should be sprinkled, lightly wet with water, then rinsed thoroughly 24 hours later. Dogs should be kept away from the area until after the final rinsing.

Skunk Odor Remover

Look for a product called "Skunk-Off" or make your own:

1 quart hydrogen peroxide
1 cup baking soda
small amount of liquid soap

Apply mixture and allow to set for several minutes before rinsing. Keep dogs away from furniture or anything else the peroxide may bleach until solution is rinsed off. (May slightly bleach coat on dark colored dogs)

Feeding The Long Eared Dog

In order to keep the ears of long eared dogs, such as cocker spaniels, from getting into moist food, slip a stretchable head band over the head and behind the ears, tucking the ears back along its neck. Usually the dog doesn't mind. Just be sure to remove the head band promptly afterwards.

Homemade Remedy For Insect Bites

(Published in "Norden News", a veterinary publication)

1 tsp baking soda
1 tsp unseasoned meat tenderizer
1/3 cup unscented household ammonia

The sting or bite area needs to be gently cleaned with warm, soapy water. Liberal amounts of the solution should be rubbed into the affected area with a soft toothbrush until the skin is reddened. Relief should be immediate.

This formula is effective against the stings or bites of bees, wasps, hornets, yellow jackets, gnats, fire ants, jelly fish, biting flies, scorpions, centipedes, caterpillars and some spiders. It works equally well on both you and your animal.

A batch generally costs under a dollar to make and may last for an entire year.

Recommended Odor Removers

"Fresh & Clean" Pet Stain & Odor Remover	(*Lambert Kay*)
"Odormute"	(*Ryter*)
"Odor Disposers"	(*Mardel)*

How To Tell When Cans Are Outdated

Here's how to read the four-digit code that are often used by companies to mark their products:

> The first number is the last digit of the year in which the food is manufactured.
>
> Example: A "1" would mean 1991 or perhaps 1981.
>
> The next three numbers are the day.
>
> Example: "024" would be the 24th day of 1991 or January 24th.

Therefore a can with the date code of 1024 was manufactured on January 24, 1991.

Save Clean-Up Time

Save clean-up time by storing spare plastic trash can liners at the bottom of the can they go with. When you remove a full bag, grab a new one to insert from the bottom of the can.

Quiet a Barking Dog

Squirt lemon juice in the mouth of a barking dog and say "Quiet" to help train him not to bark. The lemon juice is bitter, but not harmful like the old "ammonia in the eyes" remedy.

Which Puppy is It?

Use a dab of colored fingernail polish on a toenail to distinguish pet quality from show quality pups, or to distinguish one or several pups from each other for medicine, those that have been sold, etc.

To Deodorize Carpet

To remove urine from a rug or carpet, sprinkle dry baking soda on the wet spot to let it soak up the moisture. Once the spot is dry, simply vacuum. The baking soda deodorizes the area.

Poison Ivy Relief

By merely stroking a dog whose fur was in contact with an ivy plant several hours previously, you can develop an irritating itch. Try applying a weak solution of chlorine bleach and water to the area. The sooner this is done after exposure, the more it seems to help. (also try vinegar)

Pet Memorial Stones

To mark the grave of your faithful departed pet, a tastefully done custom memorial stone is available from the following source. The stone is cut from solid riverstone granite and ranges in size from 5 to 9 inches wide depending upon the name you have engraved up to 12 letters or numbers. Allow 4 to 6 weeks for delivery. Cost runs about $36 plus shipping & handling.

Seasons
P.O. Box 64545
St. Paul, Minnesota 55164-0545

Pet Fabric for Sewing

Unique purebred designs hand silk-screened on 100% cotton cloth. Purchase by the yard or in hand-crafted items. Catalog $1

Dogs By The Yard
P.O. Box 341
Portsmouth, Rhode Island 02871

Herbicide That Is Safe For Pets

Without endangering pets, children or wildlife, you can now rid your garden or yard of weeds. An all-natural herbicide, called "Sharpshooter", produced by Safer, Inc., attacks weeds with an overdose of naturally occurring fatty acids. these biodegradable fatty acids are not harmful to people and all traces disappear.

Cleaning The Air With Plants

To help remove toxic pollutants from the air in the kennel area, living plants can significantly reduce the levels of indoor contaminants found in the average building. The fumes given off by wood, carpeting, insecticides, oil based paints, cleansers, tobacco smoke and other chemicals used in the kennel may produce headaches, itchy eyes, stuffy noses and fatigue.

Plants somehow absorb pollutants and then release oxygen through pores in their leaves and microorganisms on their roots.

The most effective and easiest to maintain include the peace lily, gerbera daisy, English ivy, bamboo, chrysanthemums, marginata and spider plants.

Placing one potted or hanging plant for every 100 square feet of floor space can significantly reduce the pollutants in the air.

Fresher Breath For Your Dogs

An all natural internal breath freshener called "Pure Breath For Pets" is available from the makers of "Breath Assure". It works through the digestive system, often the source of breath odors instead of the mouth.

Breath is sweetened within 30 minutes after swallowing the capsule(s).

This product is available in small quantities at Kmart, Petco, Petsmart, etc. For larger quantities contact:

PureBreath For Pets
26025 Murreau Road
Calabasas, CA 91302

(Approximate cost $19.95 for 250 capsules)

Waterbeds For Ailing Dogs

If your dog is suffering from arthritis or simply old age, a waterbed would provide warm insulation from cold hard floors. The warmth would also be ideal for puppies. The mattress cover is puncture resistant and the frames are solid. It can be used unheated in the summer for cooling comfort.

One you might try is called "Natural Sleep". Contact them at 1-518-785-3986 or on the internet at www.naturalsleep.com

More Tips To Try

When mailing a package during inclement weather, rub a white candle over the address on the outside of the package to help seal it from any moisture.

To make bandages on your injured pet easier to remove, use a hair dryer to heat the tape from a distance for a few seconds to make the adhesive soften.

A hair dryer, set on low, can be used to dry out sutures or a wound that is moist and healing too slowly.

After trimming your dog, clean up the tiny hairs that have fallen everywhere by spraying a little hairspray on a rag or paper towel and while it's still sticky using it to wipe up the mess.

A dab of petroleum jelly will help protect your dogs paws before going out into ice and snow.

As a substiture for flying insect spray killer, use hairspray to immobilize them. The gumminess of the spray on their wings causes them to fall.

Kitty litter makes a wonderful deodorizer for boots and shoes. Simply fill the end of a stocking or sock with the kitty litter, tie the end off and slip down into the shoes overnight.

A temporary kennel for traveling can be made by inverting a laundry basket over another basket and tying the handles together.

Clean scissor blades with a quick swipe of nail polish remover on a tissue.

To get the "kennel" broom back into shape, stretch a large rubber band a few inches above the bottom of the broom.

To vacuum around an area that has small items that may inadvertently be sucked into the vacuum bag, simply cover the end of the nozzle with a piece of nylon stocking. (Also a great way to find a small item you've lost such as a needle or contact lens)

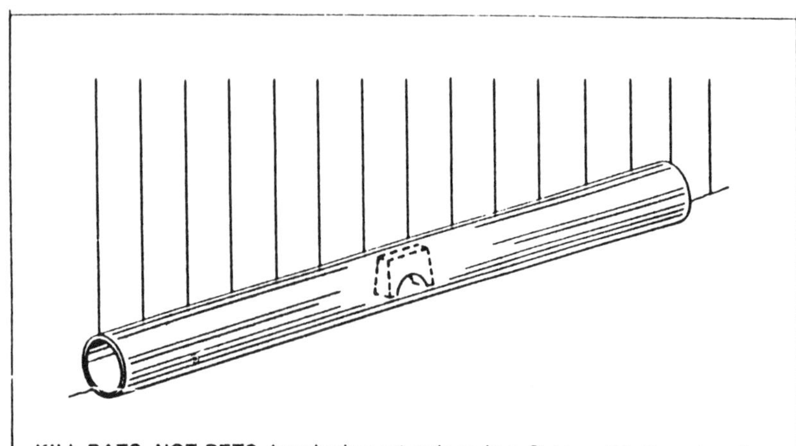

KILL RATS, NOT PETS, by placing rat poison in a 2′-long, 3″-diameter pipe. Jason Tesch, Fonda, Iowa, says it keeps pets away from the poison.

Something To Think About

The pig industry in American should be of great interest to dog breeders. For one, the money spent on pig research far exceeds any amount ever spent on other small animals. How does this help us? Think about how similar the pig is to dogs. Why can't we use the results of pig research to further our own. Many ideas can be copied from the pig producer pertaining to equipment, supplies and health updates, etc.

Microwaves Reduce Chilling

According to an article in an issue of "Hogs Today" magazine, animal scientist Doug Morrison is experimenting with microwaves to help keep baby pigs from getting chilled. Microwaves heat food from the inside out. So why not heat a chilled baby pig (or pup) the same way. Though they're not suggesting we "pop" the pup into the kitchen microwave, they are experimenting on microwaves in general, using a power setting much lower than microwave models we use at home. According to Morrison, the low microwaves do not hurt them, and prove to be an efficient way to keep them warm.

With microwaving you can reduce the air temperature in a building, keep air moving and still keep the animals warm. This may be the heat concept of the future, and sooner than we think.

Fetal Position & Sex Drive Linked

The University of Missouri did a study on the link between fetal position in utero and sex drive in piglets.

The position of a piglet in a sow's uterus was determined to be important to reproductive ability as an adult. Scientists reported that a baby pig developing inside a sow's uterus absorbs sex hormones from neighboring fetuses. Those piglets positioned between two females had a much higher sexual activity as they grew up. Gilts (female piglets) born from all-female or nearly all-female litters seem to be the most sexually active. Gilts from nearly all-male litters won't be as reproductively efficient. They may also be more aggressive and have irregular heat cycles.

Could this be an important clue to the reproducing capability of future breeding stock in our dogs? It might be worth keeping a few extra notes on our litters to see if pups from nearly all-female litters turn out to be the best breeders.

Do Your animals Do Better in Natural Light?

Studies done at the department of biology at Loyola University indicate that guppies, fish that give live birth to their young, produced 80% females and 20% poorly colored males when raised under "cool white" fluorescent tubes, whereas under natural sunlight the male/female ratio was 50/50.

Similarly, laboratory rats raised under "pink" fluorescent lights produced fewer offspring, were more aggressive, cannibalistic, irritable, died younger and were prone to getting cancer.

In pumpkins grown under "cool white" fluorescent tubes, the plants produced the male pistillate but not the female staminate. When the "cool white" tubes were replaced with "daylight white" tubes, the pumpkin vines produced only the female staminate.

Special Problems

From time to time, dog owners experience problems with their animals that require additional research to come up with solutions. The following list is arranged by category of expertise, providing you with an address to write for additional information.

Allergies, (including skin & hair disorders caused by allergies)

The Academy of Veterinary Allergy
Rural Route 1, Box 113-E
Williston, Florida 32696

Animal Behavior Problems

The American Society of Veterinary Ethnology
Building 31, Room 4D30
National Institute of Health
Bethesda, Maryland 20205

(Briefly explain your pet's problem so you can be put in touch with an expert who's knowledgeable about that particular problem.)

Bone & Joint Problems

The Veterinary Orthopedic Society
Box 6129
Salt Lake City, Utah 84106

Cancer

The Veterinary Cancer Society
Comparative Oncology Unit
Veterinary Teaching Hospital
Colorado State University
Fort Collins, Colorado 80523

Eye Diseases and Disorders

The American College of Veterinary Ophthalmologists
Dean McGee Eye Institute
608 Stanton L. Young Drive
Oklahoma City, Oklahoma 73104

Heart Disorders & Diseases

A network called Cardiopet makes it possible for your pet's heart to be monitored via a phone-line hookup. Then your veterinarian can consult directly with a board-certified cardiologist. If your vet doesn't participate in this system, suggest that he or she call 1-800-347-8300 for the name of the nearest Cardiopet practitioner.

Internal Medicine

The American College of Veterinary Medicine
620 North Main Street
Suite C-1A
Blacksburg, Virginia 24060

(Be sure to ask for an internist since this board also certifies other specialists.)

Kidney Stone Problems

Minnesota Urolith Center
College of Veterinary Medicine
University of Minnesota
St. Paul, Minnesota 55108

Nervous System Disorders

The American Veterinary Neurology Society
Department of Physiology and Pharmacology
College of Veterinary Medicine at Auburn University
Auburn, Alabama 36849

Surgery

The American College of Veterinary Surgeons
Executive Secretary
College of Veterinary Medicine
University of Illinois
SAC, No 1008
West Hazelwood
Urbana, Illinois 61801

Teeth & Gum Problems

The American Veterinary Dental Society
110 N. Orchard Street
Boise, Idaho 83706

Vet Newsletter

Vetinfo Digest
P.O. Box 476
Cobbs Creek, Virginia 23035

Keep up with the latest in veterinary health care info. A monthly compilation of new product info, new treatment options, serious health care problems, etc.

$25 per year in U.S.
$30 per year International Delivery

Hot Line Support For Grieving Pet Owners

A telephone support hot line is sponsored by the School of Veterinary Medicine at the University of California, Davis.

(530) 752-4200 M-F 6:30 till 9:30 pm PT

Animal Poison Control Center - 24 hour emergency

Credit Card Users: Call (800) 548-2423 or
(888) 426-4435

$30 per case, no extra charge for follow-up calls. Must use Visa, MC, Discover or American Express

If you don't have a credit card:
Call (900) 680-0000

$30 per case. The charge will appear on your phone bill instead.

Schools of Veterinary Medicine

Auburn University, School of Veterinary Medicine, Auburn, Alabama 36849

University of California, School of Veterinary Medicine, Davis, California 95616

Colorado State University, College of Veterinary Medicine and Biomedical Sciences, Fort Collins, Colorado 80523

Cornell University, New York State College of Veterinary Medicine, Ithaca, New York 14853

University of Florida, College of Veterinary Medicine, Gainesville, Florida 36201

University of Georgia, College of Veterinary Medicine, Athens, Georgia 30602

University of Ilinois, College of Veterinary Medicine, Urbana, Illinois 61801

Iowa State University, College of Veterinary Medicine, Ames, Iowa 50011

Kansas State University, College of Veterinary Medicine, Manhattan, Kansas 66502

Louisiana State University, School of Veterinary Medicine, Baton Rouge, Louisiana 70803

Michigan State University, College of Veterinary Medicine, East Lansing, Michigan 48824

University of Minnesota, College of Veterinary Medicine, St. Paul, Minnesota 55103

Mississippi State University, College of Veterinary Medicine, Mississippi State, Mississippi 39762

University of Missouri, College of Veterinary Medicine, Columbia, Missouri 65211

North Carolina State School of Veterinary Medicine, Raleigh, North Carolina 27607

Ohio State University, College of Veterinary Medicine, Columbus, Ohio 43210

Oklahoma State University, College of Veterinary Medicine, Stillwater, Oklahoma 74078

Oregon State University, School of Veterinary Medicine, Corvallis, Oregon 97331

University of Pennsylvania, School of Veterinary Medicine, Philadelphia, Pennsylvania 19104

Purdue University, School of Veterinary Medicine, West Lafayette, Indiana 47907

University of Tennessee, College of Veterinary Medicine, Knoxville, Tennessee 37901

Texas A&M University, College of Veterinary Medicine, College Station, Texas 77843

Tufts University, School of Veterinary Medicine Boston, Massachusetts 02111

Tuskegee Institute, School of Veterinary Medicine, Tuskegee, Alabama 36088

Virginia Tech and University of Maryland, Virginia-Maryland Regional College of Veterinary Medicine, Blacksburg, Virginia 24061

Washington State University, College of Veterinary Medicine, Pullman, Washington 99163

University of Wisconsin, School of Veterinary Medicine, Madison, Wisconsin 53706

Pattern Inheritance

Color

Dominant Factors	Recessive Factors
Black	All other colors
Solid color	Ringneck Pattern
Solid Color	Mostly white
Ringneck	Mostly white
Black & Tan	Tri-color
Black & Tan	Liver & Tan
Black & Tan	Red (type I)
Red (type II)	Black & Tan
All colors	Albino-white
All colors	Dark-eyed white
Brindle	Tan
Black & Brindle	Black & Tan
Lemon-black nose & dark eyes	Lemon-pink nose & light eyes
Ticking	Non-ticking
Merling	Tri-color
Merling	Black & Tan
Sable	Black & Tan
Sable	Cream
Red	Cream

Leg Length

Dominant Factors	Recessive Factors
Short Legs (imperfectly)	Long Legs
Long Legs	Short Legs (cockers)

Dominant Factors	**Recessive Factors**
Eye Color	
Brown Eyes	Yellow Eyes
Brown Eyes	Pearl Eyes
Coat Characteristics	
Short Hair	Long Hair
Wire Coat	Smooth Coat
Coarse Hair	Fine Hair
Sparse Coat	Dense Coat
Straight	Curly
Miscellaneous Inheritance Patterns	
Dewclaws	No Dewclaws
Stub Tail (imperfect)	Long Tail
Straight Tail	Curly Tail
Glaucoma	Normal Sight
Shorter Ears	Longer Ears
Mental Aptitudes	
Open Trailing	Still Trailing
Chop Voice	Drawling Voice
High head carriage	Low head carriage
Smiling	Non-smiling
Bird Interest	Lack of Bird Interest
Water Going	Nonwater group
Quartering	Straight Line Hunting

The Internet

If you are not already "internet friendly" you're missing out on half of the fun of running a business!

You don't have to be a whiz kid to buy a basic computer system for around $1,200 and subscribe to an internet provider for between $15 - $20 per month for unlimited usage. The costs have come way down in recent years, making it one of the cheapest forms of information gathering, peer communicating and advertising that you can possibly find. If you're a technical sort of person, go for a regular PC. If you're scared to death of a computer, go for a MacIntosh. I personally use a Mac and absolutely love it!

You're never too old to learn or too dumb to comprehend the internet.....you simply need to find an avid computer "hound" that can help you set up your system for you and help you along the way. Call your local high school and speak with them about paying a knowledgeable student to come help you after school or on weekends. They are usually thrilled at the aspect of making some spending money and showing you their expertise. You'll find that the employees of internet providers are usually much too busy to offer much assistance in your home.

There are question & answer sites with online veterinarians, you can check out the Web Page ads that other breeders are using, locate breeding studs and bitches, locate missing pets, keep up-to-date on new products, order any book you want at a discount, communicate by e'mail instantly, advertise your own dogs and services and to put it simply......the sky's the limit!

Just do it!

Index

Index

Index

Index